WILD
Virginia

Help Us Keep This Guide Up to Date

Every effort has been made by the authors and editors to make this guide as accurate and useful as possible. However, many things can change after a guide is published—trails are rerouted, regulations change, techniques evolve, facilities come under new management, and so on.

We would love to hear from you concerning your experiences with this guide and how you feel it could be improved and kept up to date. While we may not be able to respond to all comments and suggestions, we'll take them to heart and we'll also make certain to share them with the author. Please send your comments and suggestions to the following address:

The Globe Pequot Press
Reader Response/Editorial Department
P.O. Box 480
Guilford, CT 06437

Or you may e-mail us at:

editorial@globe-pequot.com

Thanks for your input, and happy trails!

WILD
Virginia

A Guide to Thirty Roadless Recreation Areas

by
Steven Carroll and **Mark Miller**

FALCON®

GUILFORD, CONNECTICUT
HELENA, MONTANA

AN IMPRINT OF THE GLOBE PEQUOT PRESS

Maps by Bruce Grubbs; © The Globe Pequot Press
All interior photos courtesy of the authors.

Library of Congress Cataloging-in-Publication Data
Carroll, Steven, 1969-
    Wild Virginia : a guide to thirty roadless recreation areas / by Steven Carroll and Mark Miller.--1st ed.
        p. cm. -- (A Falcon guide.)
    ISBN 0-7627-2315-7
    1. Outdoor recreation--Virginia--Guidebooks. 2. Wilderness areas--Virginia--Guidebooks. 3. Virginia--Guidebooks. I. Miller, Mark, 1957- II. Title. III. Series.

GV191.42.V8 C37 2002
917.5504'44--dc21   2002020633

Manufactured in the United States of America
First Edition/First Printing

Dedication

To Cindy and Gina
For all your support and encouragement

STATEWIDE OVERVIEW MAP

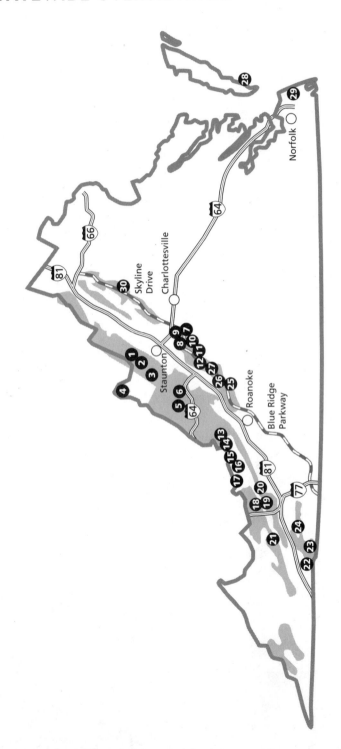

CONTENTS

ww Canoe

EAST COAST

Kayak

Kayak

SHENANDOAH NATIONAL PARK

MAP LEGEND

Interstate		Powerline	
U.S. or State Highway		Pipeline	
County or Forest Road		Mountain/Peak	9,782 ft.
Unimproved Road	143	Elevation Point	9,782 ft. ×
Railroad		Campground	△
Trail, Trailhead or Parking Area	T	Shelter	
Appalachian Trail		Picnic Area	⟊
Virginia Highlands Horse Trail		Ranger Station	
Other Trail		Boat Launch	
Bushwhack		Mine	⚒
Pass or Saddle		Cabin or Building	▪
Bridge		City or Town	○ Glasgow
Lake, River, Falls		Orientation	N
Marsh or Wetland			
Spring		Map Scale	0 0.5 1 Miles
Wilderness, National Park, or Wilderness Study Area Boundary		State Boundary	KENTUCKY VIRGINIA
Roadless Area			

ACKNOWLEDGMENTS

Writing a hiking guide might be the best job in the world. Preparing a guide to be published, however, ranks a little farther down the ladder. Through the many forms of this book, and the many phases of the process, several people have been invaluable to us. Our staff editors at The Globe Pequot Press—Jeff Serena, Shelley Wolf, and Himeka Curiel—pointed us in the right direction and followed this guide through to completion. Our copy editor, Karen Elliot, made our words clear where they were confusing. The cartographers made our rough maps smooth. Lynn Cameron, Mike Dawson, and Rob Reardon compared our trail data against their own expert knowledge. Peter Kirby supplied us with valuable information on some hard-to-find places. The first line of reviewers included Michelle Elmore, Bill Miller, and Madelyn Miller. While wilderness brings solitude and escape from people, the path invariably returns us to our cities and towns for work and our daily lives. It has been an honor spending a portion of this time working with these people. We can only hope our paths cross again.

We also give special thanks to the following groups: The Wilderness Society for its efforts to preserve America's dwindling resource of wilderness, the Appalachian Trail Conference and the many volunteers who maintain the premier "wilderness trail" in Virginia, the Forest Service for its efforts to manage Virginia's wildlands and for providing guidance where the roads ended, and the U.S. Geological Survey for the maps that keep us on our way.

INTRODUCTION

Virginia's Wilderness History

When Europeans arrived in North America, what they found in their land of opportunity was wilderness, a vast wilderness with virtually no end. In their day, this provided an escape from an oppressive Europe. The new continent's uncharted lands were the setting for an epic adventure, a stage for the discovery of the human spirit and the sculpting of the American ideal. In time the wilderness gave way to the town and the pasture. These symbols of progress grew as our nation's wildlands receded, and our country developed into an unyielding sea of civilization. As this sea threatened to overtake the islands of backcountry that remained, we began to protect America's heritage of wilderness.

On September 3, 1964, President Lyndon Johnson signed into law the Wilderness Act. The act was the result of decades of work by men the likes of Aldo Leopold and Bob Marshall, who in 1935 helped to found the Wilderness Society. Leopold, a former Forest Service employee, decided in 1924 to manage 540,000 acres in New Mexico as the Gila Wilderness Reserve. This was the first time in our country's history that wilderness had been managed as a recognized resource. Over the next several decades, support for the preservation of wilderness grew, and in 1949 a proposal was made to Congress to create a national wilderness system. The signing of the act guaranteed to all an enduring resource of wilderness for years to come. The act defined wilderness as " . . . an area where earth and its community are untrammeled by man, where man himself is a visitor who does not remain." The act established that wilderness areas would be devoted to the public purposes of recreational, scenic, scientific, educational, conservational, and historical uses. It also established the National Wilderness Preservation System (NWPS) and immediately entered into the system all lands that were previously managed as wilderness. Provisions were made for adding areas to the system, and the Forest Service was given a window of time to complete studies on other areas.

Although the Wilderness Act legally defines wilderness and how it will be protected, each person has his or her own personal reason for loving and experiencing Virginia's wildlands. Wilderness allows us an adventure, a chance to discover and test our limits. Pristine nature grants us an escape from an oppressive and increasingly demanding society. Wildland can rejuvenate the soul and energize the spirit. Many hikers need the respite that wilderness offers, a chance to "recharge the batteries" of human nature. Wilderness has value far beyond the land itself or the physical resources on that land. It affects us in ways no other aspects of our domesticated lives can.

Wild Virginia is a guide to the most pristine areas in Virginia. Virginia has dedicated sixteen wilderness areas in national forests totaling 89,863 acres. Add to this 82,260 acres in eleven units in Shenandoah National Park for a total of 172,123 acres of federally designated wilderness in twenty-six units. Although hiking is by far the predominant use of these areas, many other forms of recreation are available. Anglers frequent the streams, horse trails are available, canoeing is a quiet and serene use, and some areas sustain cross-country skiing. Wilderness visitors should remember that *mechanized* travel is prohibited in federally designated wilderness. This includes the use of bicycles. Bicycles can, however, be used in roadless areas that are not designated wilderness. Please respect and abide by this rule. There are plenty of nonwilderness miles in the national forests where bicycles are perfectly acceptable. Hunting is allowed and is a popular use in virtually all of the areas in this guide, except for lands held by the Nature Conservancy and within Shenandoah National Park. Although this guide is not a hunting guide, for your safety we do ask that you know when hunting seasons begin and end in the wilderness areas you plan to visit. Also, follow the precautions listed below in the Preparedness and Safety section.

As our nation's population increases and as demand for resources and space grows, Virginia's wildlands become more and more threatened. Roadless areas along the Atlantic seaboard are already much smaller than their western counterparts. With such high population densities in the East, it is important to protect and preserve our vanishing resource of wilderness. Although Virginia holds 174,550 acres of federally designated wilderness, consider that there are more than 420,000 acres in sixty-six inventoried roadless areas in Virginia's national forests that are not protected by wilderness designation. The key to protecting our wildlands is education and involvement. It is our hope that *Wild Virginia* will encourage more individuals to become involved in the idea of wilderness. When legislation arises to cut forests, construct roads, or develop areas on our wildlands, if more people have experienced these natural places, then more people will come to their defense. We hope that you will learn about, hike in, and enjoy Virginia's wildlands, and, when necessary, defend them. We thank you for letting *Wild Virginia* take you into the outdoors.

Zero Impact and Wilderness Ethics

Zero Impact is a philosophy of outdoor use that has become the standard for responsibly enjoying the outdoors. The idea behind it is to minimize impact on the land and the natural flora and fauna. This is especially important in Virginia's wilderness areas because, by definition, they are places where "the imprint of man's work is substantially unnoticeable." There are six basic principles of zero- and low-impact camping. By following these guidelines as closely as you can, you will ensure an enduring resource of wilderness for years to come.

Chronology of Wilderness Legislation
Important to Virginia

1964: The Wilderness Act was signed into law, establishing a system for adding lands to the National Wilderness Preservation System. The act also called for a review of roadless Park Service lands of 5,000 acres or greater, setting the stage for wilderness designation in Shenandoah National Park.

1975: The Eastern Wilderness Act designated the James River Face as wilderness. The act also determined that land that was once logged, cut, or otherwise severely altered by humans could still be considered for wilderness designation if that land had subsequently returned to a natural state. This was an important determination for eastern states, where nearly all lands had been logged, most in clear-cut fashion, in the nineteenth and early twentieth centuries.

1978: The Endangered American Wilderness Act determined that areas that were still within "sight and sound" of civilization were not disqualified from wilderness consideration. This was very important in the well-populated East because very few acres are completely out of "sight and sound" of some type of civilization.

1979: RARE II, Roadless Area Review and Evaluation, reviewed roadless areas in the eastern states and recommended lands for inclusion in the National Wilderness Preservation System. As a result of RARE II, President Carter recommended 15.1 million acres to be designated wilderness, paving the way for wilderness legislation in each state.

1984: The Virginia Wilderness Act of 1984 designated ten areas in Virginia as wilderness and established four others as wilderness study areas. Wilderness areas designated were Beartown, Kimberling Creek, Lewis Fork, Little Dry Run, Little Wilson Creek, Mountain Lake, Peters Mountain, Ramsey's Draft, Saint Marys, and Thunder Ridge.

1987: The Virginia Wilderness Act of 1987 included the four wilderness study areas established in the 1984 act in the National Wilderness Preservation System. Wilderness areas designated were Barbours Creek, Shawvers Run, Rich Hole, and Rough Mountain.

2000: The Virginia Wilderness Act of 2000 added The Priest and Three Ridges to the Virginia Wilderness Preservation System.

KNOW WHERE YOU'RE GOING AND WHAT YOU'RE DOING. This seems like basic common sense, but many hikers go out every weekend knowing very little about the area, terrain, or trail they're hiking. Hikers leave the trailhead without a map and without ever hearing a local weather report. It might be a cliché, but the Boy Scouts are right on: Be prepared. Pick up a map and look at the contour lines. Can you do that 20-mile loop or will 2,000 vertical feet in 2 miles slow you down a little? Think about the time of year and time of day you're hiking. The dawn-to-dusk hike you completed last summer will take you until after dark in the winter. Do you have a flashlight? How about proper clothing? The list could go on and on. The bottom line is that wilderness is rugged and not easily accessed. Mountain rescue involves a lot of manpower and a lot of time. Impact to the environment will take a back seat to saving a human life. Be responsible for yourself and ensure your own safety on the trail.

HIKE ON TRAILS AND CAMP IN CAMPSITES. Use of Virginia's outdoor resources is increasing every year. Hiking on established trails and camping in established campsites concentrates impact to certain areas and minimizes impact to the whole. Trails generally travel to the most interesting landmarks, and most trails are dotted with usable campsites. When hiking a trail, do not cut switchbacks. This causes serious erosion problems. Besides, saving a few steps out of several miles will not be noticeable. Some of Virginia's wildlands don't have established trails, and some adventurous hikers like bushwhacking better than trail hiking. It's true that sometimes bushwhacking is necessary and sometimes it's just plain fun, but the idea is to make it an extreme exception. Before attempting any bushwhack, think it through to minimize impact.

Campsites are located throughout the wildlands, generally along streams, near vistas, and almost always near the trail. Camping in previously used campsites benefits the hiker and the wilderness. The hiker benefits because established campsites are there for a reason: The area is usually the best spot nearby for a camp, the ground is level, a stream is nearby, and there is room for a tent and a place to cook. The wilderness benefits because impact is concentrated in small areas rather than dispersed throughout the wilderness. If a site looks unused and is attempting to recover, don't camp in it. If you must camp in a new area, make sure the ecosystem is durable enough to recover. Pitch the tent on hard ground or in a meadow, and move your tent every other day.

USE STOVES WHENEVER POSSIBLE AND LIMIT USE OF FIRES. Unfortunately, in today's low-impact camping world, the time of the campfire is nearly over. Campfire rings scar the land, are slow to decay, and are eyesores to other hikers. Camp stoves, on the other hand, pack up clean and leave no trace of their presence. They cook with higher, more controllable temperatures. Few campers who build a campfire use it for cooking anyway, but rather build it for

View of the Brushy Mountain panhandle.

aesthetics. Admittedly, the campfire has its place in the hearts of camping romantics. The light from a campfire, though, has a tendency to create a tiny
"room" of light, effectively shutting you off from anything beyond it. Spending an evening at camp without a fire allows your eyes to adjust to the darkness, allows better opportunities for seeing the creatures of the night, and
allows you to become part of the environment. Finally, and most obviously,
fires can be dangerous, to both humans and the wilderness. It takes years for a
forest to recover from the damage of one forest fire. Often, during dry times
of the year in Virginia, fires are banned altogether. If a fire must be built, place
it in an established campfire ring at an established campsite. Make sure there
is a water source nearby for dousing the fire when you're done. When visiting
Virginia's wilderness, however, where minimum impact is so very important,
pack in a camp stove and think twice about building a fire.

PACK OUT WHATEVER YOU PACK IN. This sounds fairly simple. The goal
is to bring out *everything* you take in. Don't take anything into the wilderness
knowing you will leave it behind. Litter is unacceptable on a city street and it
certainly is on a trail.

**PROPERLY DISPOSE OF HUMAN WASTE AND ITEMS THAT YOU CAN'T
PACK OUT.** There are entire books written on the subject of proper disposal
of human waste. Some minimum-impact campers subscribe to the idea of
packing out human waste too. It is true that in some ecosystems decay occurs
at an extremely slow rate, making this philosophy appropriate. Although packing out human waste is a lower impact way of camping, in most cases simply
burying waste is acceptable. The basic idea is to dig a hole well away from a
water source. No backpacker, hiker, or any type of outdoor user should be
without a trowel. After doing your business, stir it up and cover it over. If it's
not buried, it's not properly disposed of.

**LEAVE THE AREA, THE LAND, ITS PLANTS, AND ITS ANIMALS UNDIS
TURBED.** Part of the definition of wilderness contained in the Wilderness Act
describes an area where "man himself is a visitor who does not remain." When
hiking in Virginia's wilderness, think of yourself as a visitor. Leave the stones
unturned and the flowers on their stems. Their beauty lies within the brief moment you experience them on the trail. Please do not feed animals, especially
bears. Remember that you are a visitor and your goal is to slip in and out without the wilderness ever noticing.

By keeping these six ideals of zero impact in the front of your mind when
you head out on a trip, you will greatly increase the quality of your outdoor
experience. While minimizing the effect you have on the environment, you
can ensure that the wilderness will remain pristine for years to come. The

Wilderness Act has given us the ability to designate lands we would like to preserve. It is up to those who use these lands to ensure they are preserved. Think of zero impact not as a high mark to strive for, but rather a minimum of care to take. It is everyone's responsibility to care for Virginia's wildlands.

Preparedness and Safety

If we can believe statistics, you're much less likely to get hurt while through-hiking the Appalachian Trail than you are while living in the city. AT hikers are safe because they spend months preparing for their trip. Safety is directly related to preparedness; the two go hand in hand. When hiking in wilderness you will be farther from a paved road than anywhere in the state. You might hike for days and not see another hiker. To be safe in Virginia's wilderness you have to be prepared for being on your own and being self-sufficient. With experience, preparedness becomes second nature and safety becomes part of the contented feeling that is the reason we love to be in the wilderness. A few natural hazards bear special consideration.

WEATHER. Weather can be a hiker's best friend or worst enemy. Summers in Virginia tend to be hot and humid, which can be very dangerous. One hazard is dehydration. While hiking, body temperature rises and fluid is lost as perspiration. If more fluids are lost than are ingested, the result is dehydration. Be sure to drink plenty of fluids—preferably water—before the hike and remember to drink more while on the trail. Look at maps to determine where water might be available, and always purify the water to ensure that it is safe to drink. Common sense dictates that a hiker should always carry an adequate supply of water.

Heat exhaustion and heatstroke are potentially life-threatening situations. Both ailments result when the body is not cooled properly. Heat exhaustion occurs first and, if not treated, can develop into its more fatal cousin, heatstroke. If extensive hiking is planned during warm weather, consult a first-aid guide on the symptoms and treatment of heat exhaustion and heatstroke.

Summer storms, especially in the higher elevations, can develop suddenly and become severe. On Mount Rogers, a posted sign warns of the possibility of rapidly changing weather. The sign states that temperatures can drop 20 degrees and wind speed can increase by 20 miles per hour in less than one hour. Severe thunderstorms in Virginia can bring with them wind speeds of more than 50 miles per hour, along with driving rain, lightning, and hail. Such storms can topple trees, cause flooding, and create other life-threatening conditions. If severe weather threatens, find shelter from the storm.

On bright days, sunburn can be a problem in both summer and winter. While not immediately life threatening, sunburn can be painful, and it can also significantly increase your risk of skin cancer. Be aware that on sunny days

A woodland view near the summit of South Mountain in the Adams Peak Roadless Area.

and even partly sunny days the risk of sunburn exists. While hiking, remember to wear a hat to protect your face and a shirt to protect your back and arms. Shirts are not completely effective at blocking the sun's rays, especially when wet. Sunblock lotions above SPF 15 are also effective in preventing sunburn.

Cold weather brings its own risks and dangers. Two cold-weather emergencies to be concerned about are hypothermia and frostbite. Hypothermia results when core body temperature is lowered by exposure and lack of food to fuel the body. If hypothermia is not treated it can lead to death. Frostbite occurs when skin is exposed to cold, and ice crystals form in the body. It usually occurs in the extremities, particularly the fingers, toes, ears, and nose, and restricts the blood flow. If hiking when the possibility of cold weather exists, consult a first-aid guide for the symptoms and treatment of frostbite and hypothermia.

Wind chill and wet weather can play a big role in both frostbite and hypothermia. Blowing wind and rain rob the body of heat. Frostbite and hypothermia can occur quickly when wind and wetness are factors. It is a good idea to carry windproof and waterproof clothing while hiking, especially in areas with exposed ridges, such as Pine Mountain and Mount Rogers.

PLANTS. Several potentially harmful plants are found in Virginia. Learning to identify these plants is the most effective way to avoid them. Poison ivy, the most common problem plant encountered while hiking, is a climbing plant found along many trails. It grows best in sunny open areas such as old clearings and trails. Poison ivy has compound leaves of three leaflets. When touched, the plant leaves a residue that causes a skin rash characterized by itchy redness and blistering. Treatment usually involves applying lotions to the affected area. In severe cases a doctor may need to be consulted. The best way to avoid the plant is to know what it looks like. After becoming familiar with poison ivy, just stay away from it.

Mushrooms are potentially dangerous as well. Although some species are edible, most are not. If you are not an expert at identifying mushrooms, do not eat them. Eating poisonous mushrooms can cause nausea, severe pain, liver and kidney failure, and even death. The best way to deal with mushrooms is to err on the side of caution and leave them alone.

Stinging nettles can also cause problems while hiking. This plant stands about 24 inches high, with toothed leaves that grow in pairs opposite each other on the stem. The leaves have bristles filled with a watery juice that can produce an intense but short-term itch. To avoid problems with nettles, wear long pants while hiking.

There are many other plants in Virginia wilderness that may cause allergic or toxic reactions. Get a field guide and educate yourself on their characteristics. Knowing the local flora is a pleasant way to enjoy the outdoors and the best way to keep safe.

ANIMALS. While hiking, it is important to remember that we are visitors to the forest. For the animals, however, the forest is their home. Although most animals in the forest are small, even the smallest animal will defend itself when threatened. Bites and scratches can transmit disease. The best way to avoid unwanted problems with animals is to leave them alone.

Animals like food and spend most of their time acquiring it. Over the years, many animals have learned that hikers represent a supply of food. On an overnight trip, place a rope over a high limb and suspend your food pack above the ground so that animals will be unable to reach the food or destroy the pack. The mental image of a bear clawing through a tent wall to get to a pack should be enough to convince anyone to hang their pack.

Two species of venomous snake, rattlesnakes and copperheads, live in the mountains of Virginia. Both will bite when threatened, and their venom can be life threatening. The best defenses against snakebite are good boots and long pants. Although there are no guarantees that a bite will not occur, proper clothing will reduce the odds. It is also important to know what the snakes look like and where they are most likely to live. When walking in their habitat, be on the lookout. In the unlikely event of a snakebite, stay calm and seek medical help quickly. If hiking solo, it is advisable to carry a snakebite kit just to be on the safe side. Having a first-aid guide and knowing the procedure for dealing with snakebites is a must.

Insects can make life miserable for wilderness visitors. Mosquitoes thrive in wet areas, and flies are ubiquitous. Bites from either usually swell slightly and itch. Scratching can lead to infection. The best way to avoid bug bites is to wear extra layers of light clothing. Insect repellent may help where bugs are especially abundant. Ticks can also be a problem. The best remedy for ticks is to look for them periodically. If bitten, remove the tick with tweezers, taking care to pinch the head and not the body. By following accepted first-aid procedures, the risk of getting disease from a tick will be lessened.

PERSONAL SAFETY. There are many general precautions to take that will make a wilderness adventure safer and more enjoyable. Let someone know where you will be hiking and when you expect to return. Know your route of travel, including total distance and level of difficulty, then assess your ability to hike the trail. You know your ability best; listen to what your body is telling you and make safety your first priority.

Always carry a map and a compass. Before entering the wilderness, learn methods of outdoor orienteering. If you become lost, you will have the skills to find your way out of the woods and back to your vehicle.

Clothing is another important consideration. Good boots are essential for protecting against turned ankles, wet feet, and a host of other minor problems that can make a hike miserable. As good as boots are, they are only as good as the socks worn inside them. Wool socks are appropriate for hiking because they stay warm even when wet. There are summer and winter socks that suit various thermal needs. Also important is a hat, which protects the head and face from sunburn, keeps the head dry in rain or snow, and prevents blowing winds from cooling the body. A lightweight windbreaker should be carried in case of severe wind; if waterproof, it can also protect against the rain. During cooler months, hikers need to take extra precautions. Carry extra clothing, even on mild days. Many a day that begins clear and sunny ends with a snowstorm. Dress in layers so that you can regulate your temperature by adding or removing a layer. Perspiration that soaks clothing will chill you when you stop to rest. Gloves and a hat protect the extremities.

Finally, the woods around Virginia are open to hunting in the fall and winter. Because the timing of hunting seasons varies from county to county, be sure to obtain a schedule from the Fish and Game Commission and plan your hikes accordingly. It is best to stay out of the woods during the general firearms season. If planning to hike during hunting season, remember to wear blaze orange and avoid bushwhacks if possible. Blaze orange might not be your preferred fashion statement, but it will reduce the chance of a hunting accident. Deer and turkey seasons are probably the most dangerous, but be aware of any type of hunting activity.

This list of suggestions is not all-inclusive, but it does cover the broad issues. The thing to remember is that if you plan ahead and use common sense, most problems will be just minor inconveniences.

How to Use This Book

This guide is a starting point for your trip into Virginia's wilderness. When planning a trip, consult the guide to get on the right track. This book describes thirty wild areas in Virginia. A state map accompanies each description to show the area's general location in the commonwealth. The guide groups wild areas into four sections: George Washington National Forest, Jefferson National Forest, the East Coast, and Shenandoah National Park. To plan a trip, consult the statewide overview map on page vi to find wild areas in the portion of the state you want to visit, then turn to the appropriate chapters to learn more about specific wildlands.

Each chapter of the guide describes an individual wild area or complex of related areas. A detailed map of the wilderness or complex is contained in each chapter. Trailheads, trails, peaks, and other features are shown on the map. The map is not, however, meant for orienteering or compass work.

An information block for each area contains quick facts, including:

Location: An area's general location in relation to a nearby city or town.

Size: Acres of land in the wilderness, roadless area, or complex.

Administration: The agency or organization responsible for managing the area.

Management status: The area's status as wilderness, nonwilderness roadless area, special management area, national scenic area, national recreation trail, nature preserve, or national park.

Ecosystems: Forest type and ecosystem classification.

Elevation range: The high and the low points in the area. The larger the difference between the high and low points, the more rugged the area will be.

System trails: Miles of trails within and bordering an area. This gives a general idea of the pristine nature and of the amount of use within an area. Generally, the more trails, the more an area is used.

Maximum core-to-perimeter distance: The greatest distance a visitor inside the wild area can be from a road. This gives a sense of how remote an area is.

Activities: Recommended activities in each area. Hiking and backpacking are available in just about all areas; canoeing and cross-country skiing are less prevalent.

Modes of travel: How you can get around. Wilderness areas don't allow bikes, but roadless areas do. Horses are allowed in some areas.

Maps: A list of USGS maps for the particular area. Most often these will be 1:24,000 scale; exceptions are noted.

Overview: This section contains various information for each area, and might include history, highlights of the area, flora and fauna, and trail information.

Recreational uses: This section gives more detailed information on recommended uses of the area. Especially popular trails will be listed, as well as particularly interesting uses. Seasonal information is included when necessary.

Most chapters describe more than one route. For each route, the following information is included:

Type of hike: Types include day hike, shuttles, overnight backpacks, horseback rides, canoe, and cross-country ski trips.

Bloodroot, *Sanguinaria canadensis,* is a short-lived wildflower in the poppy family.

Trail name: Gives the name of the main trail or trails that will be traveled.

Distance: The length of the hike described.

Difficulty: Hikes are rated as easy, moderate, or strenuous.

Topo maps: The USGS maps that cover the area to be hiked.

How to get there: Detailed driving directions to trailheads are provided. Use these directions in conjunction with maps in this guide, USGS maps, and state road maps.

This information is followed by a detailed description of the hike. We might stay away from the most popular hikes in order to avoid overuse, but generally, the trips are to the most interesting or most scenic sections of the area.

A Word on Virginia's Colorful Names

The Appalachians have a strong regional flavor all their own, and in a book such as this, that flavor comes through in the language of landscape and place. A river or stream, for instance, is commonly called a creek, but Virginians also know them as runs, forks, coves, branches, and drafts. A mountain may also take a variety of names, usually descriptive of its shape: ridge, crest, peak, summit, knob, and—when the trees give way to low bushes, grasslands, or rock on the summit—bald.

For proper names of landmarks, towns, and other places, we have followed the usage on official maps and signs as well as local custom.

The Appalachian Trail

The Appalachian Trail runs through the heart of many of Virginia's wildlands. Each year the AT attracts scores of through-hikers attempting to hike its 2,144-mile length, from Maine to Georgia, in one hiking season. As you might expect, the AT sees even more use from casual walkers, day hikers, and short-trip backpackers. The trail travels 536 miles through some of the most wild and beautiful environments Virginia has to offer. Virginia hikers know that the trail is well marked and easy to follow, a result of the volunteer efforts of the various Appalachian Trail Conference clubs. These clubs maintain the AT, countless side trails, and trail shelters. They also maintain accurate mileage data for the trails. We thank all of the volunteers for their efforts. If you would like to become involved with an AT club, or would like to know more about the trail, please contact the Appalachian Trail Conference at the address and phone number listed below. As well as work trips, AT clubs also have a full schedule of fun outdoor activities. It's not all work and no play.

Appalachian Trail Conference
P.O. Box 10
Newport, VA 24128
(540) 544–7388

George Washington National Forest

Little River Roadless Area 1

Location: 19 miles northwest of Staunton, Virginia.
Size: 27,248 acres.
Administration: USDAFS George Washington National Forest, Dry River Ranger District.
Management status: Nonwilderness roadless area.
Ecosystems: Eastern deciduous forest.
Elevation range: 1,600 to 4,400 feet.
System trails: 45 miles of maintained trails plus many miles of old roads in various states of decay.
Maximum core-to-perimeter distance: 4.5 miles.
Activities: Hiking, biking, horseback riding, fishing, and hunting.
Modes of travel: Foot, bike, and horseback.
Maps: Dry River District map; Palo Alto-VA, Reddish Knob-VA, Stokesville-VA, and West Augusta-VA 1:24,000 topo maps.

OVERVIEW: Little River Roadless Area is a rugged region on the eastern flank of Shenandoah Mountain. Elevations here range from 1,600 feet on the Little River in the southeastern corner to 4,400 feet on the eastern slope of Reddish Knob, the second highest point in the George Washington National Forest. A hike to the summit is a worthy challenge for any hiker. Interlacing mountain streams surrounded by steep ridges characterize the area. A good example is the Little River, which is flanked by Buck Mountain, Hearthstone Ridge, Timber Ridge, Big Ridge, and Shenandoah Mountain. The region protects the upper reaches of the North River and Little River, both of which lie in the Shenandoah River watershed.

Animal life abounds in this remote region. Hikers might see black bears, white-tailed deer, bobcats, raccoons, foxes, and squirrels. In fall and winter, several different types of woodpeckers and sapsuckers can be heard calling through the woods. Turkey and grouse are also represented in large numbers, and plant life is abundant. There are many different species of wildflowers and understory trees.

The trail system of the Little River area is extensive. Most of the trails are well maintained and easy to follow. The Wild Oak National Scenic Trail, by far the most popular, is a 25.6-mile loop trail that passes through the Little River Roadless Area as well as portions of the Ramsey's Draft Wilderness and its potential roadless additions. Each major ridge sports a trail along its crest.

LITTLE RIVER ROADLESS AREA

1

No views

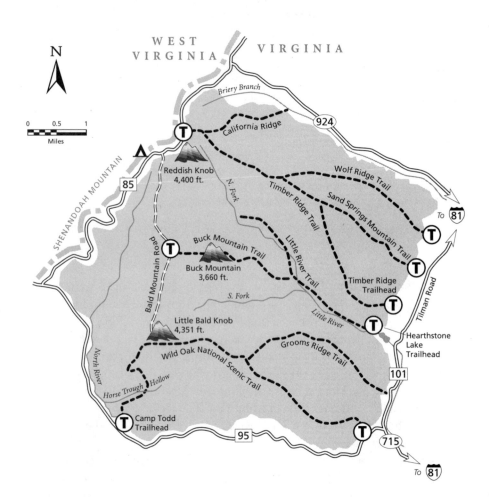

By combining this trail with old roads and some bushwhacking, visitors can find almost endless opportunities for loop hikes. In all, there are about 45 miles of trails within the roadless area.

RECREATIONAL USES: The Little River area offers many different types of recreational activities. The extensive network of trails offers many different loops for all hiking abilities. Whether looking for a day hike or an extended backpack trip, the Little River has the loop. Mountain biking is popular on several trails designated specifically for this use, the most notable of which are the Sand Springs Trail and the upper portion of the Timber Ridge Trail. Linking these trails with Bald Mountain Access Road and Forest Road 85 creates several excellent loops for bikers. Hunting is another major activity within the boundary of this large roadless area. The Little River area, nearby Ramsey's Draft, and surrounding roadless areas form a huge expanse of black bear habitat and prime black bear hunting country. Other wild game, such as white-tailed deer, turkey, and grouse, is also represented in large numbers.

Day Hike

Wild Oak Trail

Distance: 6.4 miles round-trip.
Difficulty: Moderate.
Topo maps: West Augusta-VA and Palo Alto-VA.

HOW TO GET THERE: From Interstate 81, about 2 miles north of Staunton, take exit 225 and turn west on Woodrow Wilson Parkway (County Road 275). Travel 5.5 miles west to US 250. Continue 14.5 miles west on US 250 to Braley's Pond Road (CR 715). Turn right on Braley's Pond Road and go 5.8 miles, passing a Wild Oak Trail sign, to a T intersection. Turn left on Forest Road 95 and drive 3 miles to a parking lot on the left.

This section of the Wild Oak Trail climbs steadily from Camp Todd at 2,400 feet to the 4,351-foot summit of Little Bald Knob. After crossing the North River, the trail bends right and enters Horse Trough Hollow. For the next mile, Wild Oak Trail parallels the creek in the hollow. After cresting a finger ridge, the trail bends left and contours along the ridge to a switchback going right. Near the left bend, a rock outcrop provides an excellent view of the North River basin.

After the switchback, the trail continues climbing to a lower summit, after which the hard climb is over. Wild Oak Trail traverses a short saddle and then begins an easy climb to the 4,351-foot summit of Little Bald Knob. On top,

Wild Oak Trail intersects with Bald Mountain Road, which crosses the ridge and runs north about 4 miles to FR 85. The summit is mostly tree covered. A short stroll down the road leads to a grassy area with a good view to the west. From here, retrace your route to the trailhead.

Overnight Backpack

Timber Ridge Trail

Distance: 14 miles round-trip.
Difficulty: Strenuous.
Topo maps: Reddish Knob-VA and Stokesville-VA.

HOW TO GET THERE: From I–81, take exit 240 for Mount Crawford. Turn west on Virginia Highway 257 and go 3.2 miles to a stoplight in Bridgewater. Turn right on VA 42/257 and drive 2.7 miles to Dayton. Follow VA 257 left and continue 12.1 miles west to Tilman Road, also known as Forest Road 101. Turn left and go 4.3 miles to a parking lot on the right.

Timber Ridge Trail begins at the base of Shenandoah Mountain and climbs to the summit of Reddish Knob, for an elevation gain of about 2,600 feet. The trail is marked with yellow blazes. Although the summit of Reddish Knob is not within the boundaries of the Little River Roadless Area, a lion's share of the trail leading to the summit is. This portion of the trail is open to hikers and horse riders.

After leaving Tilman Road (FR 101), the trail follows a relatively flat grade until it reaches a dry creek bed, then begins to climb moderately. About 1.5 miles from the trailhead, the trail skirts a small game pond on the right and a good flat area for camping. Continue to climb; for a short distance the grade is steep. At 3 miles the Sand Springs Mountain Trail joins on the right. The Sand Springs Mountain Trail is open to mountain bikes, as is Timber Ridge Trail from here to the summit of Reddish Knob. A right on the Sand Springs Mountain Trail leads back to Tilman Road, for a 7.4-mile loop option.

To continue on to Reddish Knob, head west on Timber Ridge Trail. A power line now mars the scenery. The trail parallels the power line from this intersection all the way to the summit. The grade continues to be moderate. At 4 miles the Wolf Ridge Trail joins on the right, about 5 miles from its trailhead on Tilman Road. If you make a loop out of Timber Ridge Trail and Wolf Ridge Trail, figure on a 10.6-mile hike, with about 1.6 miles of that on Tilman Road.

Timber Ridge Trail continues up the ridge at a moderate grade. At 6.5 miles the California Ridge Trail joins on the right. This trail drops off the ridge to

Little River Roadless Area.

the Briery Branch, but it effectively ends at a private property line; public access is prohibited. Instead, stay left on Timber Ridge. The trail passes through a ribbon of rocks, then climbs easily to the Reddish Knob Summit Road. Turn left on the road to climb to the 4,400-foot summit. The panoramic view is tremendous, with the Shenandoah Valley stretching northeast and the mountains of West Virginia fading to the western horizon.

Day Hike or Overnight Backpack

Buck Mountain Trail and Grooms Ridge Trail Loop

Distance: 15.9 miles.
Difficulty: Strenuous.
Topo maps: Palo Alto-VA, Reddish Knob-VA, and Stokesville-VA.

HOW TO GET THERE: Follow the directions for the Timber Ridge Trail. At the intersection of VA 257 and Tilman Road (FR 101), turn left and drive 5 miles to the Little River sign. Turn right and proceed 0.7 mile to Hearthstone Lake.

This loop begins at Hearthstone Lake and traverses the summits of both Buck Mountain and Little Bald Knob before dropping back to Tilman Road. The hike can be done as a very long day hike or an overnight backpack. From the parking area at Hearthstone Lake, walk back up the road to the Little River Trail at an earthen barrier. Beyond the barrier, the trail is somewhat hard to follow. Generally, it parallels the right side of the Little River. Once in the woods it becomes easier to follow, running on an old roadbed along the river. Where the trail becomes indistinct again, watch for red and blue blazes painted on the trees. Just before the third creek crossing, a USGS benchmark shows an elevation of 1,987 feet.

After the third creek crossing, the trail forks. A sign at the junction gives the distance to the end of the North Fork as 4 miles and to the summit of Buck Mountain as 1 mile. Backpackers may want to take a side trip up the North Fork of the Little River about 3 miles to an excellent spot to camp along the creek.

To continue the main loop, take the left fork, the Buck Mountain Trail, which is marked with yellow blazes. The trail switchbacks right, staying to the right of a dry creek drainage, and begins to climb a steep ridge. Portions of the trail are covered with windfall, which makes walking difficult. After four steep climbs, the trail reaches the top of tree-covered Buck Mountain. A sign gives the distance back to Hearthstone Lake as 4 miles and the distance to Bald Mountain Road as 1 mile. The trail drops to a saddle and then climbs to join Bald Mountain Road. In a field at the intersection with Bald Mountain Road, a USGS benchmark gives the elevation as 3,885 feet.

Turn left on Bald Mountain Road and continue 2.1 miles south to the junction with Wild Oak Trail near the 4,351-foot summit of Little Bald Mountain. The total hiking distance to this point is about 7.1 miles. At the junction, take the left fork of the Wild Oak Trail, which begins a long descent along Chestnut Ridge to the Grooms Ridge Trail. Initially, the descent is steep and rocky, but after about 1.4 miles the grade moderates somewhat and hiking becomes easier. The trail passes through mountain laurel and scrubby oaks into a parklike forest just before the junction with the Grooms Ridge Trail. Here the Wild Oak Trail splits right and continues its descent 4.6 miles to FR 95.

To close the loop with a short walk along the road to Hearthstone Lake, follow the Grooms Ridge Trail straight as it begins a 4-mile descent to Tilman Road. Initially, the descent is steady, but it is punctuated by one short, steep climb over the crest of a small knoll. After this summit, the trail continues downhill, reaching Tilman Road (FR 101) about 13.5 miles into the hike. Turn left (north) and walk 2.4 miles back to the trailhead at Hearthstone Lake.

Ramsey's Draft Wilderness

Location: 22 miles west of Staunton, Virginia.
Size: 19,290 acres.
Administration: USDAFS George Washington National Forest, Deerfield Ranger District.
Management status: 6,519-acre wilderness area with a 12,771-acre perimeter of nonwilderness roadless land.
Ecosystems: Eastern deciduous forest.
Elevation range: 2,200 to 4,282 feet.
System trails: 37 miles.
Maximum core-to-perimeter distance: 3.8 miles.
Activities: Hiking, backpacking, fishing, and cross-country skiing.
Modes of travel: Foot, cross-country skis.
Maps: USDAFS Ramsey's Draft Wilderness map; Deerfield District map; MacDowell-VA, Palo Alto-VA and WVA, and West Augusta-VA 1:24,000 topo maps.

OVERVIEW: With high, rocky peaks above 4,000 feet, a crisp, clear stream with plenty of brook trout action, and a healthy big-game population, it's not hard to understand why Ramsey's Draft is a popular destination for outdoor enthusiasts of many persuasions. The area contains more than 36 miles of trails, with trailheads along the northern, southern, and eastern borders. Aside from the fishing and the hunting, the draw of Ramsey's Draft is undoubtedly the trees. At the upper reaches of the draft lies one of the largest stands of virgin timber in the southeast. Enormous pine, oak, and hemlock convey an almost parklike feeling; the forest is like no other in the state of Virginia. High ridges and south- and east-facing slopes harbor stands of pitch, table mountain, and Virginia pine. Stands of virgin hemlock, oak, tulip poplar, and pine can be found along the banks of Ramsey's Draft.

Weekends during the warmer months attract hikers and anglers to the draft, but opportunity for solitude can still be found along the ridge tops and on weekdays. In winter, yours will likely be the only fresh tracks in the snow.

The lands within and around Ramsey's Draft have significance in American history as well as in natural history. The area was purchased by the federal government in 1913 and has been managed as wilderness since 1935. Coincidentally, the Wilderness Society was launched in January of that same year. The lower portion of the area had been used as a Civilian Conservation Corps camp in the 1930s, and the CCC was responsible for creating many of the

views

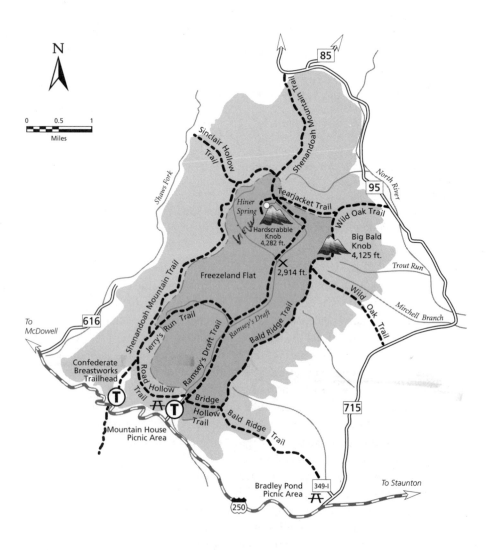

trails that are used today. During the Civil War, Stonewall Jackson's army camped near Mountain House Picnic Area, prior to the battle at McDowell. Mountain House was a tollbooth and a favorite rest stop for travelers along the Parkersburg-Staunton turnpike before the Civil War. Confederate soldiers constructed the breastworks at the crest of Shenandoah Mountain as a stronghold to keep Union forces out of the valley and the turnpike open.

RECREATIONAL USES: Ramsey's Draft is one of the most widely used of all of Virginia's wilderness lands, in part because of its location in the more densely populated northern half of the state. Hiking and backpacking are popular, and the Ramsey's Draft Trail bears the brunt of activity. Spring and fall bring out fly fishers who like to test their skills against the whims of the draft's healthy native brook trout. In the fall, the hikers and anglers share use with hunters. The area is popular for hunting deer, bear, wild turkey, and squirrel. The many trailheads along the perimeter of the roadless area facilitate hunter access to the more remote ridges. A welcome winter activity becoming more popular along the Shenandoah Mountain Trail is cross-country skiing. In winter the chances for solitude are excellent.

Day Hike

Ramsey's Draft Trail

Distance: 14 miles round-trip.
Difficulty: Moderate.
Topo maps: West Augusta-VA and Palo Alto-VA and WVA.

HOW TO GET THERE: From Interstate 81 just north of Staunton, take exit 225. Drive 5.5 miles west on Woodrow Wilson Parkway (Virginia Highway 275) to US 250. Continue 19.8 miles west on US 250 to the Mountain House Picnic Area on the right. Turn right into the picnic area, cross a small bridge, and drive 0.1 mile north to the trailhead parking lot.

Ramsey's Draft Trail is the most popular hike in the wilderness area and one of the most popular on Virginia roadless lands. The trail closely follows the draft, eventually reaching a large stand of virgin timber at the northern end of the trail. Expect to meet many other hikers and anglers on the trail, especially on spring weekends.

The easy hike is made more difficult by past flood damage. Although the draft floods almost every year, severe damage from a major flood in 1995 is still evident. Slowly make your way along the draft, taking time to notice damage to the hemlocks caused by the hemlock woolly adelgid, a type of aphid. The adelgid is a serious threat to the virgin timber farther up the draft.

Brook trout, Virginia's only native trout, tend to be smaller than Rainbow or Brown varieties. This specimen is on the large side.

About 2.3 miles from the trailhead, a sign marks Jerry's Run Trail, which goes left and up the ridge to Shenandoah Mountain Trail. Stay on Ramsey's Draft Trail as it continues up the draft, meandering east of Freezeland Flat. At 4.3 miles the trail arrives at the upper forks of Ramsey's Draft at an elevation of 2,914 feet according to a USGS benchmark nearby. Follow the trail up the right-hand fork and into a unique and beautiful forest, an unrivaled example of untouched old growth. The trees are massive and the understory is sparse.

At 6.2 miles the trail meets Tearjacket Trail, with Hiner Spring nearby to the west. In another 0.3 mile the summit trail for Hardscrabble Knob goes left. Follow this trail for about 0.5 mile as it wraps west and south to the 4,282-foot rocky summit. From the top, enjoy beautiful views of Crawford Mountain, Great North Mountain, even farther south to House Mountain near Lexington, and Sharp Top and Flat Top.

To return to the trailhead, retrace your steps down Ramsey's Draft Trail, or consider a longer loop, following either Shenandoah Mountain Trail to the west or Bald Ridge Trail to the east. Shenandoah Mountain Trail follows its namesake south and re-connects with the Ramsey's Draft Trailhead via a short walk down Road Hollow Trail. Bald Ridge Trail follows the Eastern Ridge south and re-connects with the trailhead via Bridge Hollow Trail.

If you have several days, plan to spend a night or two camping along the trail and exploring side trips. Several campsites are available along the length of Ramsey's Draft Trail, and water is nearly always available. Please remember, though, that Ramsey's Draft Trail is a popular hike that is sometimes loved to death. To increase your opportunity for solitude, and to minimize environmental impact, plan your hike for times of the year when visitation is low, such as winter months or weekdays rather than weekends.

Overnight Backpack

Rim Hike

Distance: 16.8 miles.
Difficulty: Moderate.
Topo maps: McDowell-VA and West Augusta-VA.

HOW TO GET THERE: See the preceding directions to the trailhead for the Ramsey's Draft Trail day hike.

The Rim Hike is a piecing together of several hikes along the ridge tops surrounding Ramsey's Draft Wilderness. The result is an overnight backpacking trip through parts of these wilds that most visitors do not see. A word to the wise: This is a ridge-top hike and water could be difficult to find. Although it is readily available at the campsite described below, be sure to carry water for the hike in.

The Rim Hike begins at the Ramsey's Draft Trailhead just north of the Mountain House Picnic Area. Walk about 100 yards north on the Ramsey's Draft Trail and turn right (east) on Bridge Hollow Trail, which immediately crosses the draft and begins climbing. The trail gains 1,100 feet of elevation over the next 2 miles before connecting with Bald Ridge Trail. Turn left and hike north on Bald Ridge Trail as it follows the ridge top about 4 miles to a junction with Wild Oak Trail near a small pond. Continue 1.6 miles north on Wild Oak Trail, traversing the 4,125-foot summit of Big Bald Knob, to Tearjacket Trail. Turn left and take Tearjacket Trail west 1.2 miles to Ramsey's Draft Trail.

The junction of Tearjacket and Ramsey's Draft Trails offers a good place to set up camp. Hiner Spring, the headwaters for Ramsey's Draft, is nearby, and short day hikes can be made to the rocky top of Hardscrabble Knob or to the heart of the virgin timber the wilderness is famous for. If you've had enough of up-and-down hiking on the ridge tops, walking out on Ramsey's Draft Trail is all downhill and shorter than finishing the Rim Hike loop.

The remainder of the Rim Hike follows Shenandoah Mountain Trail, which joins Ramsey's Draft Trail just north of Hiner Spring. Go left (west) and follow Shenandoah Mountain Trail south 6 miles to Road Hollow Trail. Turn left again and walk 2 miles east on Road Hollow Trail back to Ramsey's Draft Trail. Turn right and walk about 0.3 mile south to the Mountain House Picnic Area and Ramsey's Draft Trailhead.

Cross-country Ski

Shenandoah Mountain Trail

Distance: 19.4 miles round-trip.
Difficulty: Moderate.
Topo maps: McDowell-VA and West Augusta-VA.

HOW TO GET THERE: From Interstate 81 just north of Staunton, take exit 225. Drive 5.5 miles west on Woodrow Wilson Parkway (Virginia Highway 275) to US 250. Continue 20.3 miles west on US 250 to the Confederate Breastworks on the right (north) side of the road, about 1.5 miles past Mountain House Picnic Area. Hike along the short interpretive trail loop to the Shenandoah Mountain Trail, which leaves the loop, heading north.

Although there are few places in Virginia that are suitable for cross-country skiing, Shenandoah Mountain Trail has seen a dramatic increase in winter activity over the past few years. Thanks to its high elevation and shelter from sunlight, snowmelt along Shenandoah Mountain Trail is slow. Snowfall in this area tends to accumulate all winter and may last well into March. Add to this the relatively easy to moderate terrain of the trail along the ridge crest and low use of the trail in winter, and the Shenandoah Mountain Trail is a rare opportunity for Virginia cross-country skiers to practice their art in virtual solitude.

Shenandoah Mountain Trail begins at an elevation of 2,900 feet and climbs only 1,100 feet in 9.7 miles. The high point is just before the intersection with Ramsey's Draft Trail. Several side trails along the way drop east and west off the ridge. Less than a mile from the trailhead, Road Hollow Trail drops south and east toward Mountain House Picnic Area. About 0.5 mile farther, Jerry's Run Trail curves east and into Ramsey's Draft Wilderness. Just under 9 miles from the trailhead, Sinclair Hollow Trail goes left (west) and provides access to portions of the roadless Ramsey's Draft Addition. From here, Shenandoah Mountain Trail climbs for another 0.6 mile before dropping to link with Ramsey's Draft Trail. Turn around before the trail starts its descent, and follow your tracks back to US 250.

Crawford Mountain Roadless Area 3

Location: 15 miles northwest of Staunton, Virginia.
Size: 9,868 acres.
Administration: USDAFS George Washington National Forest, Deerfield Ranger District.
Management status: Nonwilderness roadless area.
Ecosystems: Eastern deciduous forest.
Elevation range: 1,660 to 3,728 feet.
System trails: 14.2 miles.
Maximum core-to-perimeter distance: 3.2 miles.
Activities: Hiking and mountain biking.
Modes of travel: Foot and mountain bike.
Maps: Deerfield Ranger District map; Churchville-VA, Elliott Knob-VA, Stokesville-VA, and West Augusta-VA 1:24,000 topo maps.

OVERVIEW: Crawford Mountain Roadless Area encompasses all of Crawford Mountain as well as the ridge to Crawford Knob. Crawford Mountain and Elliott Knob form the crown of the far western portion of Augusta County. The region is located within the Ridge and Valley Province of Virginia. As with many of the big mountains of western Virginia, Crawford Mountain begins with a gentle slope and then becomes steep and rugged near the summit. There are several rock outcrops near the summit and along Crawford Knob that provide good views to the north and west.

Several small creeks find their origins high on the mountain. Many of these creeks have interesting names, such as Stony Lick, Wood Draft, Jehu Hollow, Coalpit Run, Spruce Lick Branch, and Dry Branch. Ironically, Dry Branch, which rises from Red Oak Spring, is the only reliable year-round source of water. In the dry months of July and August, visitors should carry ample drinking water.

This remote, high region is covered almost entirely by forest and provides an excellent habitat for black bear. In fact, Crawford Mountain is considered one of the best black bear habitats outside of Shenandoah National Park.

RECREATIONAL USES: The major recreational use of the Crawford Mountain area is hiking. There is an extensive trail network. Some of the trails, such as the Crawford Mountain Trail south of the summit and the Chimney Hollow Trail, are well maintained and easy to follow. Others, notably the northern end

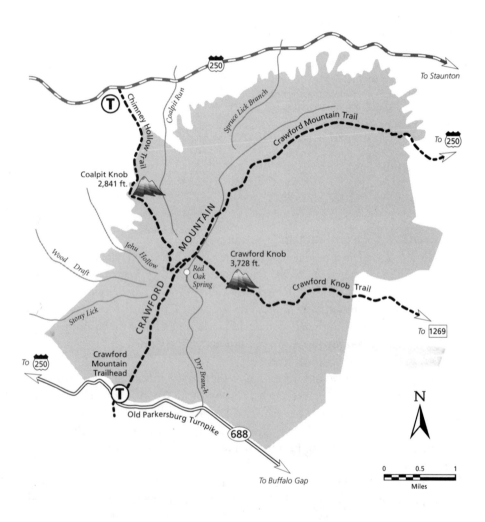

of the Crawford Mountain Trail, are less distinct and harder to follow. Mountain bikers test their skills on the many steep trails within the roadless area. White-tailed deer and black bear find refuge on the rugged slopes of the mountain, making it a favorite of hunters.

Day Hike

Crawford Mountain Trail

Distance: 5 miles round-trip.
Difficulty: Easy to moderate.
Topo maps: Elliott Knob-VA and West Augusta-VA.

HOW TO GET THERE: From Staunton, drive west on US 250. At the junction of US 250 and Virginia Highway 42 in Churchville, turn left on VA 42. Travel 6 miles to Old Parkersburg Turnpike (County Road 688), turning right at the stop sign in Buffalo Gap. Turn right on CR 688 and go 3.9 miles west to the mountain gap. Parking is on the left; the Crawford Mountain Trail begins on the right (north) side of the road.

After crossing an earthen barrier, the Crawford Mountain Trail follows an old road north. The trail is marked with yellow diamond-shaped blazes. After a switchback, take the left fork at a trail junction. Now the trail really begins to climb. Second-growth red oak, chestnut oak, and hickory dominate the overstory. The understory is composed of small dogwood, serviceberry, and mountain laurel.

The trail is marked by a series of four steep climbs followed by short descents. The second climb begins about 1.3 miles from the trailhead. A huge red maple marks the end of this climb. After the fourth steep section, the Crawford Mountain Trail crests the summit ridge. The Chimney Hollow Trail joins on the left, 2 miles from the trailhead. Red Oak Spring is located a little to the east of this junction. The Chimney Hollow Trail descends the west flank, crosses over Coalpit Knob, and continues a total of 3.6 miles to the trailhead on US 250.

Past the trail junction, the Crawford Mountain Trail continues along the ridge another 0.5 mile and meets Crawford Knob Trail (Forest Trail 487). Bear right (east) and cross a short saddle before climbing almost to the summit of Crawford Knob. Past the knob the trail begins to descend, crowded by mountain laurel and scrub oak, which makes hiking difficult. From here, the distance to Forest Road 1269 is about 3.4 miles. Most hikers prefer to turn around on Crawford Knob and retrace their steps to the trailhead on CR 688.

Laurel Fork Special Management Area   4

Location: Northwest Highland County, about 9 miles north of Monterey, Virginia.
Size: 9,938 acres.
Administration: USDAFS George Washington National Forest, Warm Springs Ranger District.
Management status: Special management area.
Ecosystems: Eastern deciduous forest.
Elevation range: 2,700 to 4,000 feet.
System trails: 23.2 miles.
Maximum core-to-perimeter distance: 3.2 miles.
Activities: Hiking, backpacking, fishing, and hunting.
Modes of travel: Foot.
Maps: Warm Springs District map; Snowy Mountain-VA and WVA, and Thornwood-VA and WVA 1:24,000 topo maps.

OVERVIEW: Hiking through red spruce forest and watching a beaver repair its dam with yellow birch branches, visitors here may stop and think how wonderful Maine is—but this is Virginia. Laurel Fork is a special management roadless area with flora and fauna unlike anywhere else in the commonwealth. Beaver ponds dot the small streams, snowshoe hares hide in the thickets, and flying squirrels do circus acts among the branches. Laurel Fork proper is a pristine mountain stream with a good reputation for native brook trout. It is also one of the headwaters of the Potomac River. The area boasts an extensive trail system, making Laurel Fork a virtual outdoor paradise.

Laurel Fork lies in western Virginia, a rural region of high winding roads and low green farmlands. The drive through these western Virginia mountains is itself a treat. Consider timing your trip to Laurel Fork to correspond with the Highland County Sugar Maple Festival held in the spring.

Although wild and roadless today, keep in mind that Laurel Fork has had a long fight to remain pristine. The wonderful patches of red spruce were once the dominant species over the entire area, but logging of the spruce in the 1920s gave northern hardwoods such as yellow birch the opportunity to take hold in the canopy. Shortly after the area was logged, the Forest Service took over its management, but reminders of lumber days are still evident in old rail grades. More recently, Laurel Fork has been threatened by long-standing mineral rights issued for more than 90 percent of the area. Backpackers and anglers

LAUREL FORK SPECIAL MANAGEMENT AREA

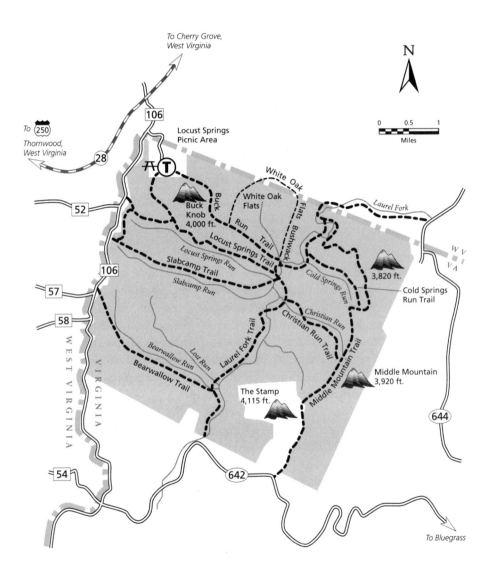

To Cherry Grove, West Virginia

N

To (250)
Thornwood, West Virginia

0   0.5   1
Miles

106

28

52

106

57

58

WEST VIRGINIA

54

Locust Springs Picnic Area

White Oak

White Oak Flats

Buck Knob 4,000 ft.

Buck Run Trail

Flats Bushwhack

Laurel Fork

3,820 ft.

Locust Springs Trail

Locust Springs Run

Slabcamp Trail

Slabcamp Run

Cold Springs Run

Cold Springs Run Trail

Christian Run

Christian Run Trail

Bearwallow Run

Lost Run

Laurel Fork Trail

Bearwallow Trail

The Stamp 4,115 ft.

Middle Mountain Trail

Middle Mountain 3,920 ft.

642

644

W V
VA

To Bluegrass

alike have applauded the designation of Laurel Fork as a special management area, but the true celebration awaits wilderness designation.

RECREATIONAL USES: By far the most widely pursued activities in Laurel Fork are hunting and hiking. There is a distinct browse line created by a large deer population. Other species found here include black bear, turkey, and squirrel. The trail system is exceptional, and many circuit hikes can be created. Camping spots are plentiful along Laurel Fork and its tributaries, as well as along ridge tops. Day hikers will enjoy the Locust Springs Picnic Area located on Forest Road 106 just off West Virginia Highway 28. Fishing is also good; the fork supports a healthy brook trout population.

Day Hike or Overnight Backpack

Locust Springs Run/Buck Run Loop

Distance: 6.2 miles.
Difficulty: Moderate.
Topo maps: Snowy Mountain-VA and WVA, and Thornwood-VA and WVA.

HOW TO GET THERE: From Staunton, drive 57 miles west on US 250 to the West Virginia border. Continue 7 miles west to the junction with West Virginia Highway 28 in Thornwood and turn right, traveling north on WV 28 about 4 miles to the sign for the Locust Springs Picnic Area. Turn right onto Forest Road 106 and follow the signs about 1.5 miles to the picnic area. The Locust Springs Trail can also be reached from the Slabcamp Trail parking area, which is another 2 miles south on FR 106. Watch for a parking area on the left. Spur trails link these two trailheads (see map).

From Locust Springs Picnic Area, walk west on the Locust Springs Trail. At about 0.3 mile, turn right as Locust Springs Trail goes south, traveling downhill. After about 0.6 mile, the trail meets the spur from Slabcamp Trailhead near the bottom of Locust Springs Run, where the canopy consists of hemlock and yellow birch. Bear to the left and steeply down to the stream to stay on the trail.

The trip downstream from here, although easy to moderate in grade, can be a difficult hike. Several stream crossings are required. Downed timber can be plentiful after hard winters, requiring hikers to crawl through it at times. This can be especially challenging with a large backpack on. The trail continues and is easy to follow. When the ridge to the right becomes covered with rhododendron, the junction with the Laurel Fork Trail is near. The ridge descends to the creek, and the Laurel Fork Trail is reached about 2.8 miles from the trailhead. A sign marks the junction. There are many sites along the banks of Laurel Fork that are perfect

Laurel Fork.

for camping. Although this hike is relatively short for an overnight trip, the reward for the quick hike in is more time in the picturesque stream valley.

To complete the circuit, turn left (north) on the Laurel Fork Trail. Within a few minutes, the Laurel Fork Trail branches right and the Buck Run Trail goes left. Follow the Buck Run Trail west about 3 miles as it climbs moderately back to Locust Springs Picnic Area.

Overnight Backpack

Laurel Fork/Middle Mountain Trail

Distance: 12.9 miles.
Difficulty: Moderate.
Topo maps: Snowy Mountain-VA and WVA, and Thornwood-VA and WVA.

HOW TO GET THERE: Follow the preceding hike's directions to Locust Springs Picnic Area and trailhead.

From ridge-top vistas to stream-side rest stops, this overnight trip leads the hiker through a cross-section of everything the area has to offer. The trail begins by following the Locust Springs Trail description (see above) to the junction with the Laurel Fork Trail about 2.8 miles from the trailhead. Set up camp

A view into West Virginia from Middle Mountain.

along Laurel Fork. The scenery is spectacular, campsites are level and easy to find, and water is plentiful.

From the junction with the Laurel Fork Trail continue north a short distance to the junction with the Buck Run Trail. Follow the Laurel Fork Trail as it branches east, crosses several streams, and follows the banks of Laurel Fork. Along the way the trail passes the Cold Springs Run Trail; stay on the Laurel Fork Trail heading north. When the stream makes a narrow U-turn at the base of a very steep ridge, the Middle Mountain Trail is near. Take a right onto Middle Mountain Trail, and follow it up the difficult ridge. The trail tops out soon enough and follows the ridge top across Middle Mountain. The Middle Mountain Trail passes through a saddle, where signs mark the upper junction with the Cold Springs Run Trail, which drops down the ridge from here. To shorten the hike, turn right and follow the trail back down to Laurel Fork.

From the junction in the saddle, the Middle Mountain Trail starts a moderate ascent, switches back to the left, and wraps around the ridge. Pass through a gate and follow the trail to a beautiful mountain meadow where a curious pile of rocks encircles a shade tree. In the past, homesteaders would clear an area for farmland. As they plowed a new pasture, they picked up the field rocks and placed them in these piles. Some gathered rocks for fences, and some just piled them in circles around the trees.

At this pasture, another sign points toward Christian Run Trail going west. Follow this trail down the ridge to Laurel Fork Trail, turn right (north) and hike downstream back to the junction with Locust Springs Trail. Retrace your route along Locust Springs Trail to the trailhead.

Option: The pasture also offers a possible side trip south along Middle Mountain toward The Stamp, the highest point in the local area. Topping the altimeter at more than 4,000 feet, The Stamp is a beautiful bald rimmed with red spruce. Unfortunately, the summit is on private property and hikers can approach only to within wishful thinking distance.

Follow the Middle Mountain Trail past a couple of side roads accessing farmland. A road to the top of The Stamp goes to the right. Shortly after this, the national forest land ends at pastureland. To get a look at the summit without trespassing, follow the road to the right over to a gate, then walk the Forest Service side of the fence line as far as you can. From here you can see the summit, stands of beautiful red spruce, and the wild mountains of Virginia and West Virginia.

To return to the campsite and complete the trip, go back to the meadow and the junction with the Christian Run Trail and follow the directions above back to the trailhead. The entire trip, including the walk to The Stamp, is just under 13 miles. The campsite welcomes tired feet and offers the reward of a good supper and a peaceful night's sleep.

An old cabin along the White Oak Flats Bushwhack.

Day Hike

White Oak Flats Bushwhack

Distance: 6.5 miles.
Difficulty: Strenuous.
Topo maps: Snowy Mountain-VA and WVA, and Thornwood-VA and WVA.

HOW TO GET THERE: Follow the previous directions to Locust Springs Picnic Area and trailhead.

White Oak Flats is a wide, flat-topped mountain on the edge of the Laurel Fork area. Although there are old logging roads to the crest, the route described here follows a trail and then bushwhacks. As with all bushwhacks, care should be taken. Bushwhacking is for adventurous hikers who enjoy exploring away from the securities of a marked trail. This hike is included as a short aside, a rugged day hike of just a few hours. The hike is also appropriate as a change of pace for someone who is spending several days camping in Laurel Fork.

The hike begins at the Locust Springs Picnic Area. Follow the Buck Run Trail on an old road out of the picnic area. It runs east on a gentle downhill grade, through a forest of tall cove hardwoods. After about 0.5 mile, the trail passes an area well gnawed by beaver. There are several ponds on the left, and some of the dams stand 4 to 5 feet high. In the meadows surrounding the ponds, small stands of red spruce have taken up residence. Past the ponds, the creek drops rapidly away from the trail, but its gurgling noises never completely disappear. About 1.5 miles from the trailhead, the trail branches off the road and becomes a path that continues down the finger ridge and then begins a series of switchbacks back to the creek. After you cross the creek on a small wooden bridge, the grade moderates. Continue downstream to the next creek crossing. It is at this point that the bushwhack begins. Instead of crossing the stream, turn left (north) and head toward the gullies.

Follow the easternmost drainage to the saddle at the ridge top, where an old cabin sits by a gravel road. To continue to the crest of White Oak Flats, follow the old logging road up the ridge behind the cabin. The flat is littered with downed timber. Travel across the top of the mountain to the southeastern end of the ridge where the mountain drops away abruptly. Work your way carefully downhill. As you descend, veer slightly to the right. This ensures that when you get to the bottom, you will link back up with the Buck Run Trail. When you reach the Buck Run Trail, turn right (west) and head uphill to the picnic area.

Rough Mountain Wilderness

Location: 17 miles northeast of Covington, Virginia.
Size: 10,131 acres.
Administration: USDAFS George Washington National Forest, James River and Warm Springs Ranger Districts.
Management status: 9,300-acre wilderness and a 1,131-acre nonwilderness roadless area.
Ecosystems: Eastern deciduous forest.
Elevation range: 1,300 to 2,800 feet.
System trails: 4 miles.
Maximum core-to-perimeter distance: 1.6 miles.
Activities: Hiking and backpacking.
Modes of travel: Foot.
Maps: James River and Warm Springs District maps; Longdale Furnace-VA and Nimrod Hall-VA 1:24,000 topo maps.

OVERVIEW: Rough Mountain is a large and rugged wilderness within rural Alleghany and Bath Counties. Although Congress set aside these 9,300 acres as designated wilderness in 1987, Rough Mountain has long been protected from development by its own rugged terrain, lack of water, and inaccessibility. Slopes are steep and dry, with poor soil consisting of high amounts of weathered slate and shale. Streams on the ridges are intermittent, and the only perennial streams—Cowpasture River on the west and Pads Creek on the east—run at the foot of the mountain.

Lack of water is a serious issue. If hiking along the Crane Trail or along the ridge top, pack in all the water you might need. The rugged terrain and dry local climate will likely demand that you increase your water intake. Remember that the only filterable water is found at the base of the mountain. From the pinnacle of Griffith Knob, it's a long way down to fill your bottle.

Accessibility is another issue. Rough Mountain is almost encircled by private property, making it difficult to find a point to start a bushwhack. The Crane Trail is the only official trail within the wilderness area, and it is less than 4 miles long, running east to west over the crest of Rough Mountain. The only other area accessible to hiking is the ridge top of Rough Mountain, starting from a forest road off of Virginia Highway 42 to the north. The hike along the ridge top is about 10.5 miles one way.

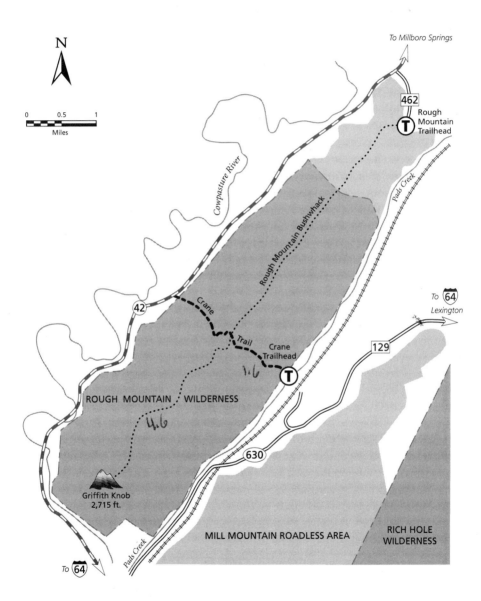

The most interesting land feature in the Rough Mountain Wilderness is also the most difficult to reach. Griffith Knob, a sharp peak at the southern terminus of Rough Mountain's crest, provides tremendous views to the east, south, and west. From the top of Griffith Knob you can see Rich Hole Wilderness, Douthat State Park, and the city of Clifton Forge. The dry ridges surrounding Griffith Knob contain an abundance of fossils, evidence that this landform was once the floor of a vast sea.

RECREATIONAL USES: Hunting is the predominant activity in this area. Open seasons for deer, bear, turkey, and small game are scattered throughout fall and winter, and another turkey season is held in the spring. Check Virginia game regulations for specific dates. Due to limited access and few trails, this area does not see heavy use from hikers. Hunters and local landowners do not expect to see hikers, so it is a good idea to wear blaze orange during the fall and early winter. Hikers interested in solitude and a true backcountry experience will find it on Rough Mountain, thanks to its limited access and lack of maintained trails. Finally, despite limited access (the west side of the river is private property), the Cowpasture River harbors fishable populations of smallmouth bass, rock bass, and perch. Also, Pads Creek along the eastern boundary holds small numbers of trout.

Day Hike

Crane Trail

Distance: 8 miles round-trip.
Difficulty: Moderate.
Topo maps: Longdale Furnace-VA and Nimrod Hall-VA.

HOW TO GET THERE: From Lexington, drive 12 miles west on Interstate 64 to exit 43. Turn north and drive 0.3 mile to a stop sign. Turn left on County Road 850, drive 0.8 mile south, and turn right onto CR 780. Go 1.7 mile north and turn left onto CR 633, which is a dirt road. Drive 4.3 miles west and turn left (south) onto Forest Road 129. Continue 6.3 miles south to a Y intersection. Take the right fork uphill and continue 1.5 miles to a small parking lot near the railroad tracks. Begin the hike by walking north along the tracks.

The Crane Trail is a relatively short hike that crosses Rough Mountain from east to west. The elevation at either end is about 1,360 feet, and the trail crosses the crest at 2,530 feet, so strong legs are an asset on this hike. There is no public access to the Crane Trail from the west. Private homes and hunting camps line Virginia Highway 42, and most of this land is posted against tres-

Griffith Knob is the dominant landmark in Rough Mountain Wilderness.

pass. Not to fear, though, as limited access means that you may have the area to yourself.

The hike begins at the parking lot on FR 129. Walk north beside the tracks about 1 mile to a railroad bridge. A Forest Service information board is located on the left (west), just past the bridge. The trail begins alongside a small creek. Initially the grade is easy, but as the trail bends right and leaves the stream, the climb grows more steep. When the trail reaches a right switchback, the ridge top is near.

A small grassy area amid hardwoods and conifers graces the ridge top at 1.6 miles. The descent of the west ridge begins with a couple of switchbacks; the trail drops gently in comparison to the steep mountainside. Pass through a ribbon of rock and then a rhododendron thicket. From this point, the trail follows a shoulder down the mountain, becoming steeper as it nears VA 42. Signs mark the wilderness boundary, your turnaround point. From here, climb back over the ridge to the parking area.

Note: The Crane Trail is a good way to shave some hiking miles off the Rough Mountain Bushwhack (see below) for those wanting to visit the Griffith Knob Area. From the east, when the ridge top is reached, turn left (south) and follow the trail description below from the Rough Mountain–Crane Trail intersection.

Day Hike

Rough Mountain Bushwhack

Distance: 21 miles round-trip.
Difficulty: Strenuous.
Topo maps: Longdale Furnace-VA and Nimrod Hall-VA.

HOW TO GET THERE: From Clifton Forge, drive about 4 miles east on Interstate 64 to exit 29. Turn north onto Virginia Highway 42 and drive 15.1 miles to a small dirt road, Forest Road 462, on the right. Turn right and go 0.2 mile to a gate. Park on the left (don't block access to the gate). Begin the hike by walking up the road beyond the gate.

The Rough Mountain Bushwhack could be the loneliest hike in Virginia. It certainly is demanding, tracing the ridgeline north to south from pinnacle to pinnacle until reaching the terminus of Rough Mountain at Griffith Knob. The views are spectacular and the soul is rejuvenated with the wildness and solitude of the mountain.

The hike begins at the Forest Service gate by the parking area. The forest is a mix of oak and poplar. A small creek to the left is your last opportunity to filter some drinking water before the long, dry climb and scramble. There is no water on the ridgeline. The beginning of the hike is along an old road that slowly gains elevation and ends after about 0.8 mile. Bushwhack to the ridge top, turn left, and head generally southwest. The slopes along the ridge top are dominated by oak and hickory to the east and laurel thickets to the west. The thickets have a ground cover of huckleberry and blueberry. About 2.6 miles into the hike, the wilderness boundary is reached. Warm Springs Mountain can be seen to the west.

The next portion of the hike involves a series of climbs along the ridge top. The ridge rises through stands of chestnut oak, pine damaged by pine bark beetle, and scrub pine. After the climb out of the scrub pine thicket, look east for views of Goshen Pass and the Blue Ridge Mountains and southeast to Rich Hole Wilderness and Pleasant Mill Ridge.

From this point, a series of steep ups and downs leads to the intersection with the Crane Trail at 5.9 miles. There is a grassy area at the intersection suitable for camping. If water is needed, turn left and follow the Crane Trail down the eastern slope 1.6 miles to Pads Creek. Depending on rainfall and the time of year, you might reach water in a feeder stream before getting to Pads Creek.

From Crane Trail, the bushwhack route continues south, climbing a short distance and then dropping steeply to a small saddle. Climb again to a high point, where your choices are to go southeast or west. Walking slightly to the west leads you to the highest point within the wilderness, an unnamed 2,800-foot peak. Turning southeast and descending slightly leads you toward Griffith Knob. After this descent there will be a gradual rise. As the peak of Griffith Knob nears, the sides of the ridge drop off steeply. From the knob, there are views to the east, south, and west. The town of Clifton Forge is visible, as is the Cowpasture River far below. Enjoy the view, but keep an eye on the time. Remember that this hike is an out-and-back and is only half done. Retrace your route to the trailhead on FR 462.

Rich Hole Wilderness/Mill Mountain Roadless Area

6

Location: 12 miles west of Lexington, Virginia.
Size: 17,326 acres.
Administration: USDAFS George Washington National Forest, James River and Warm Springs Ranger Districts.
Management status: 6,500 acres of designated wilderness, plus a 10,826-acre nonwilderness roadless area.
Ecosystems: Eastern deciduous forest.
Elevation range: 1,200 to 3,300 feet.
System trails: 12 miles.
Maximum core-to-perimeter distance: 1.5 miles.
Activities: Hiking, backpacking, fishing, and hunting; mountain biking in roadless area.
Modes of travel: Foot in wilderness; mountain bike and horseback in roadless area.
Maps: James River and Warm Springs District maps; Longdale Furnace-VA, Millboro-VA, and Nimrod Hall-VA 1:24,000 topo maps.

OVERVIEW: Waiting just west of Interstate 64 between Lexington and Clifton Forge, Rich Hole Wilderness is one of the most accessible of Virginia's wildlands, yet its remote location in rural Alleghany County makes it one of the loneliest. The Rich Hole and Mill Mountain areas combine for a total of more than 17,000 roadless acres. Trails here offer scenic views and streamside naps. What they don't offer are loop opportunities or access to the heart of the area. To see the interior, be prepared to bushwhack, which, fortunately, is relatively easy.

The major forest type in this area is a mix of oak and hickory. There are also stands of hemlock and yellow and white pine. Dogwood and black gum occupy the understory along the slopes. Several timber stands in the Mill Mountain Roadless Area have been harvested in the past twenty years. The area is prime black bear habitat, and a quiet hiker has a good chance of seeing a bruin or two. Several large rock outcrops punctuate the eastern slope of Brushy Mountain, visible from I–64. North Branch and Alum Springs run nearly the length of Rich Hole, and a drinking source is rarely hard to find. As always, purify water from any backcountry source before drinking it.

30

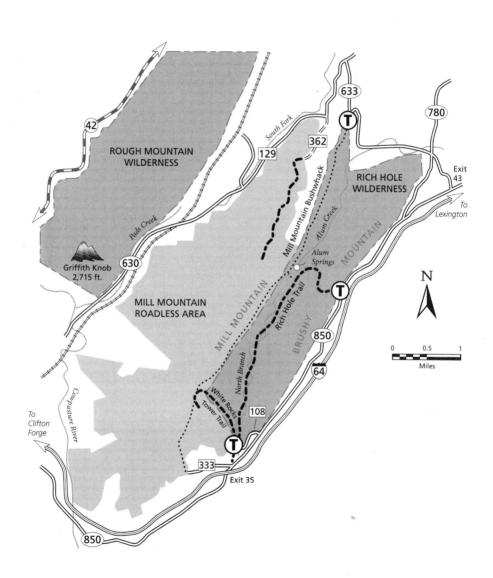

ROUGH MOUNTAIN
WILDERNESS

RICH HOLE
WILDERNESS

Exit
43

To
Lexington

South Fork

Pads Creek

Griffith Knob
2,715 ft.

MILL MOUNTAIN
ROADLESS AREA

Alum Creek

Alum
Springs

Mill Mountain Bushwhack

Rich Hole Trail

MILL MOUNTAIN

BRUSHY

North Branch

White Rocks
Tower Trail

To
Clifton
Forge

Capasture River

Exit 35

N

0   0.5   1
Miles

42

633

780

362

129

630

850

64

108

333

850

RECREATIONAL USES: By far the most popular activity in Rich Hole is hunting. During deer season, County Road 850, which runs parallel to I–64 along the eastern boundary of the wilderness, is dotted with campers and recreational vehicles. Bear, turkey, and squirrel are also hunted here. Trout swim in North Branch and South Fork, and also in Simpson Creek, along CR 850. These streams receive very little fishing pressure. Horseback riding is gaining popularity in the Mill Mountain Roadless Area. Rock outcrops, notably on Brushy Mountain, offer climbing potential. Hiking here is on the rise, but is mostly limited to day hikes along Rich Hole Trail. The potential for solitude is great, especially for off-trail backpackers.

Shuttle Day Hike

Rich Hole Trail

Distance: 6 miles one way.
Difficulty: Moderate.
Topo maps: Longdale Furnace-VA and Nimrod Hall-VA.

HOW TO GET THERE: *Upper Rich Hole Trailhead*—From Lexington, drive 12 miles west on Interstate 64 to exit 43. Turn right at the bottom of the exit ramp and drive 0.3 mile north to County Road 850 (old Virginia Highway 60). Turn left on CR 850 and drive 2.6 miles west to the trailhead and parking lot on the right just after the gap.

Lower Rich Hole Trailhead—From Lexington, drive 19 miles west on I–64 to exit 35. Turn right (east) on CR 850. Go 1.3 miles and turn left (northwest) onto Forest Road 108, which is gated and might be locked. If the gate is locked, the hike begins here. If not, drive another 1.3 miles west and north to a Rich Hole Wilderness sign next to a small boulder. This marks the trailhead. You can also reach the lower trailhead from the upper trailhead by continuing 5.7 miles south on CR 850 to FR 108.

From the lower trailhead on FR 108, Rich Hole Trail follows North Branch upstream between Mill Mountain and Brushy Mountain. The well-marked, well-traveled, easy-to-follow trail crosses North Branch several times as it gradually climbs to a high shoulder on the northern end of Brushy Mountain. At this point, about 4.7 miles from the trailhead, the trail turns south and drops rapidly into the Potato Patch, an old homestead where orchard trees still grow. Past the Potato Patch, the trail continues plummeting down the ridge. It soon skirts a rock outcrop with a view of North Mountain before descending to the upper trailhead on CR 850.

The North Branch drains the western slope of Brushy Mountain and the eastern slope of Mill Mountain.

Shuttle Day Hike or Overnight Backpack

Mill Mountain Bushwhack

Distance: 10.5 miles one way.
Difficulty: Strenuous.
Topo maps: Longdale Furnace-VA, Millboro-VA, and Nimrod Hall-VA.

HOW TO GET THERE: *Northern Trailhead*—From Lexington, drive 12 miles west on Interstate 64 to exit 43. Turn right and go 0.3 mile north to CR 850. Turn left and drive 0.8 mile west on CR 850. Turn right on CR 780 and drive 1.7 miles north to CR 633. Turn left and drive 3.1 miles west on CR 633 to a small parking lot and unmarked trailhead on the left.

White Rocks Tower Trailhead—From Lexington, drive 19 miles west on I–64 to exit 35. Turn right (east) on CR 850. Go 1.3 miles and turn left (northwest) onto Forest Road 108, which is gated and might be locked. If the gate is locked, park here. If not, drive another 1.3 miles west and north to a Rich Hole Wilderness sign next to a small boulder that marks the trailhead.

South End of Bushwhack—From FR 108, drive 0.7 mile south on CR 850 and turn right (west) onto FR 333. Drive 3.2 miles west to where the road dead-ends.

The hike from north to south along the ridge of Mill Mountain is a mix of rugged bushwhacking and following sometimes indistinct hunting and game trails. It offers a glimpse of true backcountry in a state dominated by development. The hike is rugged at both ends, as the ridge is scaled and descended, but the balance is fairly easy, by bushwhacking standards. Also, the bushwhack can be ended early by crossing the saddle between Mill Mountain and Brushy Mountain to join Rich Hole Trail.

Although the 10.5-mile bushwhack can certainly be completed as a day hike, the rugged nature of the hike may make some hikers wish they had brought camping gear. If opting for an overnight, the best camping can be found in the saddle between Mill Mountain and Brushy Mountain. Keep in mind, however, that the nearest water sources from the saddle are either a bushwhack to Alum Springs or a hike down Rich Hole Trail to North Branch. To complete this hike, you need to arrange a shuttle with a car waiting at your planned exit trailhead.

The full hike described here begins from the north on CR 633 and heads south along the ridge of Mill Mountain until it ends at the dead end of FR 333. From the northern trailhead on CR 633, cross a gate on an old road going south. Where the road forks, take the left fork toward the ridge top. The trail crosses several small meadows and passes stands of dwarfed, blight-infected chestnut. Soon the road ends, but the trail continues up the ridge.

Along the ridge top, other trees are also fighting a battle. The pines here are having difficulty with a pine bark beetle infestation. The ridge crest narrows and comes to a rock outcrop. Continue to the left of these rocks. Oak and hickory now dominate the forest, which gradually gives way to another rocky ridge crest with views of Brushy Mountain to the east. If you're ready to end the bushwhack, keep an eye on Brushy Mountain. When you are even with the mountain's highest elevation, you can turn left and cross the saddle between the two mountains. This puts you on Rich Hole Trail about 1.8 miles from the Upper Rich Hole Trailhead and 4.3 miles from the Lower Rich Hole/White Rocks Tower Trailhead on FR 108.

Continuing the bushwhack along Mill Mountain, you will eventually meet White Rocks Tower Trail, which offers another early end to the bushwhack. Drop left (east) on White Rocks Tower Trail about 1.5 miles to reach FR 108.

The final leg of the bushwhack actually follows another trail south along the ridge. Within about 0.5 mile, a rock outcrop affords an excellent view of North Mountain to the south and east. The trail continues its long descent, finally ending at FR 333.

Three Ridges Wilderness

Location: 20 miles south of Staunton, Virginia.
Size: 4,702 acres.
Administration: USDAFS-George Washington National Forest, Pedlar Ranger District.
Management status: Wilderness area.
Ecosystems: Eastern deciduous forest.
Elevation range: 1,000 to 3,970 feet.
System trails: 13 miles of maintained trails.
Maximum core-to-perimeter distance: 2.25 miles.
Activities: Hiking, camping, and photography.
Modes of travel: Foot.
Maps: Pedlar Ranger District map; Big Levels-VA, Horseshoe Mountain-VA, Massies Mill-VA, and Sherando-VA 1:24,000 topo maps.

OVERVIEW: Three Ridges Mountain lies on the eastern side of the Blue Ridge Mountain and provides a commanding view of both The Priest and the piedmont of Virginia. This roadless area is underlain by the Blue Ridge Complex, and hosts a wide variety of sedimentary, igneous, and metamorphic rocks. Rising almost 3,000 feet from the foothills, the area is characterized by extremely steep slopes and narrow V-shaped valleys. There are many large rock outcrops along the summit ridge that provide outstanding views to the northeast and southeast.

Scarlet oak and chestnut oak dominate the dry rocky slopes, but many other tree species can be found in the overstory and understory. In the sheltered coves of Harpers Creek and Campbells Creek, tall cove hardwoods such as black cherry, tulip poplar, basswood, ash, and sugar maple thrive. Some of the trees attain enormous sizes. In the old fields, thicket stands of locust are present.

Steep canyon walls hem in the creek bottoms. Huge boulders lie pell-mell along these creeks, forming innumerable small waterfalls and pools. Native trout find refuge in the small pools of Harpers Creek and Campbell Creek, which flow into the Tye River. Little Creek and Reeds Creek flow to the Rockfish River.

The remote nature of the Three Ridges Mountain provides a home for many game and nongame animal species.

Vicw'

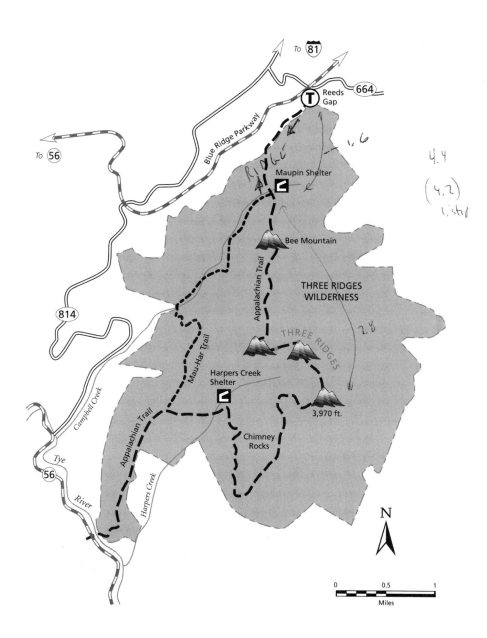

To (81)

664

Reeds
Gap

Blue Ridge Parkway

To (56)

RIDGE

1.6

4.4

(4.2)

Little

Maupin Shelter

Bee Mountain

Appalachian Trail

THREE RIDGES
WILDERNESS

THREE RIDGES

2.8

814

Mau-Har Trail

Harpers Creek
Shelter

Appalachian Trail

3,970 ft.

Campbell Creek

Chimney
Rocks

Tye

56

River

Harpers Creek

N

0   0.5   1
Miles

RECREATIONAL USES: Three Ridges is one of the prime hiking and backpacking destinations in Virginia. Ten miles of the Appalachian Trail traverse the rugged landscape of Three Ridges. The Potomac Appalachian Trail Club maintains two traditional AT shelters within the wilderness boundaries. Located 5.8 miles apart, they provide excellent shelter for an easy overnight trip. Numerous rock outcrops afford ample opportunities for beautiful pictures and taking a rest while climbing Three Ridge's steep slopes. Combining the AT with Mau-Har Trail creates one of the best loop trails in the state of Virginia. The tough ascent along the Mau-Har Trail is more than offset by the scenic beauty found along Campbell Creek.

Anglers find plenty of challenges applying their skills against the native trout that inhabit the numerous small pools of Harpers Creek and Campbell Creek.

Day Hike or Overnight Backpack

AT/Mau-Har Trail Loop

Distance: 12. 8 miles.
Difficulty: Strenuous.
Topo maps: Big Levels-VA, Horseshoe Mountain-VA, Massies Mill-VA, and Sherando-VA.

HOW TO GET THERE: From Waynesboro, drive 3 miles east on Interstate 64 to the Afton exit and turn south on the Blue Ridge Parkway. Drive about 13.5 miles south to the crossroads of Reeds Gap and watch for the Appalachian Trail sign on the left (east). Park here. The trail leaves the Blue Ridge Parkway on the east side of the road heading south.

The AT/Mau-Har Trail loop begins at the parking area on the parkway. At the AT trailhead, hike south toward Virginia Highway 56. The AT begins with an easy climb through an open meadow. Shortly after entering the woods, a sign gives the distance to Maupin Fields (2 miles), Harpers Creek (8 miles), and VA 56 (10 miles). Beyond the sign, the trail starts a serious climb to the crest of a ridge. The tops of many trees show significant damage from winter storms and gypsy moth infestation.

There are two steep climbs before cresting the ridge, then the AT drops to the east side of the ridge and descends to Maupin Fields. There are three switchbacks during the descent. The trail leads to a saddle and a small clearing. A sign at this junction indicates the distance back to Reeds Gap (1.6 miles), and ahead to Three Ridges summit (2.8 miles), Harpers Creek (5.8 miles), and VA 56 (8.3 miles). A right leads to the Maupin Shelter and the Mau-Har Trail. Continue straight as the AT follows the old road.

The next 0.6 mile is a steep climb to a high knoll, followed by a descent to a saddle and then a steady climb toward the summit of Three Ridges Mountain. After cresting the ridge to the summit, there are two large rock outcrops with tremendous views. The Priest and the summit of Three Ridges Mountain dominate the skyline at the second outcrop. There is a flat region before the final climb to the summit of Three Ridges Mountain, which is covered by small, stunted chestnut oak and provides a good view of the piedmont. There is a sign at this point with the distance back to Reeds Gap (4.2 miles), Harpers Creek (3.2 miles), and VA 56 (5.8 miles).

The AT makes a right turn on the summit and then starts its descent off Three Ridges Mountain. It begins with sixteen switchbacks to Chimney Rocks, followed by four more switchbacks to a short flat section. Another eleven switchbacks follow, then the trail descends along the southwest ridge to the Harpers Creek Shelter, where water is available. The shelter is located on a wide, flat expanse that is dominated by tall, straight cove hardwoods.

Past the shelter, the trail crosses Harpers Creek and climbs a finger ridge. At the trail junction with the Mau-Har Trail, a sign gives the distance to VA 56 (1.8 miles), Harpers Creek Shelter (0.8 mile), and the AT (3.0 miles).

Turn right onto the Mau-Har Trail, marked with blue blazes. Initially, the trail is flat and easy as it follows an old road grade. At the end of the road, a climb of seven switchbacks leads to a finger ridge. The trail passes to the west side of the ridge and begins a descent to Campbell Creek, a small creek lined by tremendous boulders. The trail climbs steeply through this boulder-strewn watershed to an old road; turn left. The grade is easy for a short distance before another moderate climb to Maupin Shelter, which has a table and privy. Water is located behind the shelter. Continue on the Mau-Har Trail about 0.2 mile to the junction with the AT, turn left, and retrace your route back to Reeds Gap.

The Priest Wilderness

Location: 18 miles northeast of Buena Vista, Virginia.
Size: 5,726 acres.
Administration: USDAFS George Washington National Forest, Pedlar Ranger District.
Management status: Wilderness area.
Ecosystems: Eastern deciduous forest.
Elevation range: 997 to 4,063 feet.
System trails: 6.2 miles.
Maximum core-to-perimeter distance: 1.8 miles.
Activities: Hiking, hunting, fishing, and biking.
Modes of travel: Foot, bicycle.
Maps: Pedlar Ranger District map; Massies Mill-VA 1:24,000 topo map.

OVERVIEW: The Priest Wilderness is a 5,726-acre wilderness area established by Congress in 2000. The Priest, a huge mountain visible for miles, dominates the area. Lying atop the Blue Ridge Complex, the region is underlain by a great diversity of rock from the three major rock types: sedimentary, igneous, and metamorphic.

The region is characterized by very rugged terrain. Steep ridges and deep V-shaped hollows are common throughout this beautiful area. These hollows contain dense thickets of rhododendron and mountain laurel. The ridges are covered with second-growth forest, while the forest floor is covered with a wide variety of understory vegetation, including blueberry, huckleberry, and many different species of fern. Cove hardwoods such as tulip poplar, maple, basswood, and hemlock form the overstory in moist, protected sites. Mountain laurel, muscadine grape, dogwood, and rhododendron dominate the understory in many places.

This pristine region is drained by several small creeks, including Crabtree Creek, Cripple Creek, and Rocky Run. Wildlife in the roadless area includes white-tailed deer, black bear, bobcat, raccoon, possum, and wild turkey. The rugged nature of the region provides ample cover for wildlife.

RECREATIONAL USES: Hiking is the main recreational use in the Priest Wilderness. The Appalachian National Scenic Trail is the only major trail located within the boundaries of this area. Fly-fishing is limited to Coxs and Cripple Creeks. Mountain biking is possible along FR 1238 and 263, which border the southwest side of the wilderness.

views

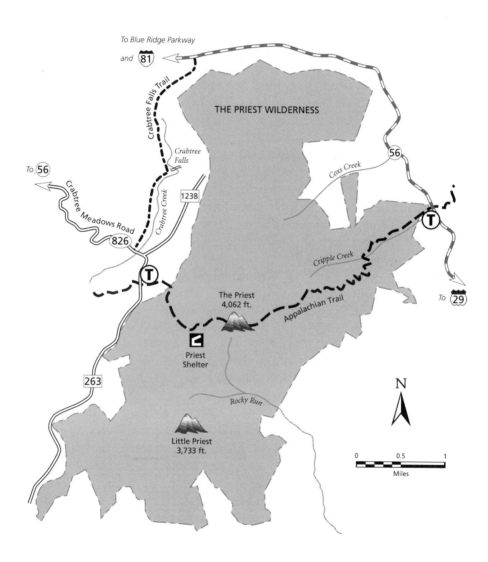

Day Hike

The Priest Shelter and Summit

Distance: 2.8 miles round-trip.
Difficulty: Easy.
Topo map: Massies Mill-VA.

HOW TO GET THERE: *From Lexington,* take Interstate 81 to exit 205. Turn east on CR 606. Travel 1.5 miles to US 11, turn left, and proceed 100 yards to Virginia Highway 56. Turn right, travel 9.2 miles, and turn right on Crabtree Meadows Road. Continue 3.8 miles to the Crabtree Meadows Parking Area. The lower parking area is 7.8 miles beyond Crabtree Meadows Road on the right.

From Lynchburg, take US 29 north to Virginia Highway 151. Turn left (north) on VA 151 and proceed 10.7 miles to VA 56. Turn west on VA 56 and continue 6.8 miles to the lower parking area on the left. To reach the upper parking area, travel 14.6 miles to Crabtree Meadows Road. Turn left and proceed 3.8 miles to the Crabtree Meadows Parking Area.

This short hike climbs to the summit of one of Virginia's 4,000-foot peaks. From the parking area, turn left on the gravel road and walk up to the junction with the Appalachian Trail. Turn left on the AT and head north. The trail follows an old road grade and is marked with white blazes. The grade is moderate as the trail climbs the north side of the ridge. After approximately 0.5 mile, a break in the trees provides a good view to the northeast and the Three Ridges Wilderness.

The AT begins to flatten out near the junction with the Priest Shelter Spur Trail, 0.9 mile from the trailhead. (The spur continues straight, drops about 200 yards, and enters a clearing where there is a shelter, a privy, a picnic table, and a spring—everything needed to have a great picnic.) Turn left on the AT, continuing the climb on an easy grade to the summit of the Priest. The forest here is composed of oak and hickory. Along the summit ridge are many rock outcrops with excellent views to the east. The 4,062-foot summit is a large rock boulder with a rock cairn on the top.

The AT continues its northward trek down to VA 56 and the Tye River Gap. The descent begins with a steep drop for approximately 0.5 mile, after which it mellows considerably. A series of long switchbacks across the front of a steep finger ridge makes the descent much easier. About midway through these switchbacks is a rock outcrop with a great view to the east. Approximately 2.9 miles from the summit, the AT crosses a small feeder creek and continues its moderate descent.

The AT follows an old road, and the creek drops sharply away from the trail. Just before reaching the parking area, 4.2 miles from the summit, the trail drops back to the creek.

If hiking this trail from Tye River Gap, it is important to note that it is rated as one of the toughest climbs (more than 3,000 vertical feet) along the whole length of the AT.

Saint Marys Wilderness

Location: 15 miles south of Staunton, Virginia.
Size: 10,090 acres.
Administration: USDAFS George Washington National Forest, Pedlar Ranger District.
Management status: Wilderness area.
Ecosystems: Eastern deciduous forest, including oak-hickory, cove hardwood forest types.
Elevation range: 1,780 to 3,640 feet.
System trails: 27 miles.
Maximum core-to-perimeter distance: 1.8 miles.
Activities: Hiking, backpacking, and camping.
Modes of travel: Foot.
Maps: Pedlar Ranger District map; USDAFS Saint Marys Wilderness map; Vesuvius-VA and Big Levels-VA 1:24,000 topo maps.

OVERVIEW: The Saint Marys Wilderness is located on the crest of the Blue Ridge Mountain. This roadless region plunges from the crest to the Shenandoah Valley. Several long ridges extend from the crest of the Blue Ridge to the west before descending rapidly. The wilderness has three high peaks within its boundary: Cellar Mountain, Bald Mountain, and Big Spy Mountain. The Saint Marys River, the major drainage for the wilderness, is fed by many smaller creeks within the drainage basin. The Saint Marys River maintains a strong flow throughout the year. Cold springs drain the western portion of the wilderness. Because of all these creeks, water is readily available. Remember to treat the water before drinking.

The forests of the Saint Marys can be divided into four major groups. The first is the oak-hickory forest, which dominates most of Virginia. A second forest type can be found on the dry slope of the steep mountain located within the wilderness. These slopes have drier tree species such as chestnut oak and Virginia pine. Tulip poplar, hemlock, and white pine thrive in the wet sheltered coves like Chimney Branch and Bear Branch. Some of these trees grow very tall. Finally, there is Big Levels, which is the home of table mountain pine and stunted chestnut oak, as well as numerous other smaller species, which endure a difficult existence in this harsh environment.

There are several interesting sites around the Saint Marys Wilderness. Because of the steep nature of the mountains and the many streams located on the sides of these mountains, small waterfalls can be seen in many places. The

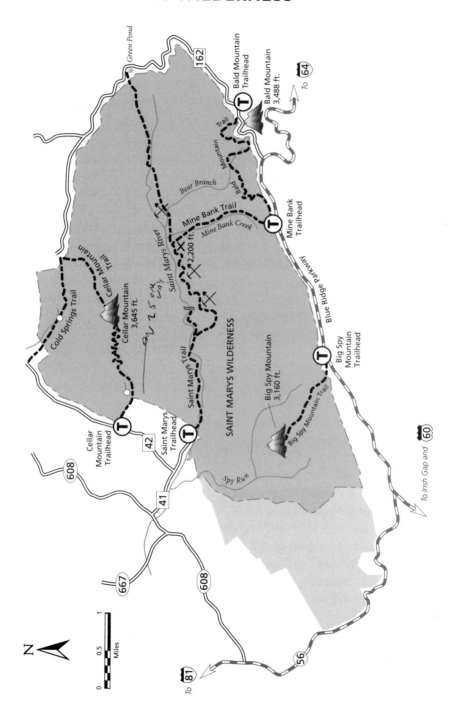

Green Pond

162

Bald Mountain Trailhead

Bald Mountain 3,488 ft.

To 64

Bald Mountain Trail

Bear Branch

Mine Bank Trailhead

Mine Bank Trail

Mine Bank Creek

2,200 ft.

Saint Marys River

Cellar Mountain Trail

Cold Springs Trail

Cellar Mountain 3,645 ft.

Saint Marys Trail

SAINT MARYS WILDERNESS

Blue Ridge Parkway

Big Spy Mountain Trailhead

Big Spy Mountain 3,160 ft.

Big Spy Mountain Trail

Cellar Mountain Trailhead

42

Saint Marys Trailhead

To Irish Gap and 60

608

Spy Run

41

667

608

56

N

1

0.5

Miles

0

81

To

Saint Marys Falls is the most popular. There are also falls along the Mine Bank Trail and in Bear Hollow.

The rocks of the Saint Marys are spectacular, making this the wilderness area for rock lovers. There are numerous rock slides and rock towers located along many of the trails. Big Levels is a huge flat region located at the top of the northern end of the wilderness. This area sports one of the few natural bodies of water in Virginia, Green Pond, located just outside the wilderness.

RECREATIONAL USES: The Saint Marys Wilderness has one of the most extensively maintained trail systems in the Virginia wilderness system. There are approximately 27 miles of trails within the wilderness or near its perimeter. These trails provide excellent access to this unique region. Although it has been declared a primitive area, the evidence of man's past is very obvious. Extensive mining activities took place throughout the Saint Marys region for many years, and the remains of those old operations are still visible today. The Saint Marys is a popular destination for hikers and campers and is usually very busy, especially around the Saint Marys Falls area. Because of this high use, camping is prohibited around the falls area.

Rock hunters and geologists find this wilderness interesting because of the various rock types that can be found here.

Day Hike

Cellar Mountain/Cold Springs Trail Loop

Distance: 6.4 miles.
Difficulty: Strenuous.
Topo maps: Vesuvius-VA and Big Levels-VA.

HOW TO GET THERE: Take Interstate 81 to exit 205, south of Staunton. Turn east on County Road 606. At the T intersection, turn left on US 11, proceed 100 yards, and turn right on Virginia Highway 56. Travel 1.2 miles, cross the South River, and turn left on CR 608. Go 2.2 miles to a yield sign. Turn right under the train trestle and continue on CR 608. Travel 0.3 mile to FR 41 (St. Marys Road) and turn right. Proceed 0.6 mile to FR 42 and turn left. The parking area is on the right, 0.8 mile from this intersection.

The trail begins at the parking area on FR 42. A Forest Service information center and a livestock gate are at the trailhead. The trail is well maintained and marked with blue blazes. The beginning of the trail is usually wet in the winter and early summer. Shortly after crossing the trail guard, begin climbing a moderate grade through a forest of mixed hardwoods and pine. A spring on

Stair-step falls along Mine Bank Trail.

A view west on the Cellar Mountain Trail.

the left about 0.5 mile from the trailhead is the last water for a few miles.

Beyond the spring the trail becomes very steep. A switchback to the left is followed by a long, steep, rocky straight stretch. At the next switchback, the Cellar Mountain Trail enters a stretch of nineteen switchbacks. There are several views of the Blue Ridge Mountains and the Allegheny Mountains to the west. Small ferns and running cedar are visible, and large anthills dot the landscape in this area.

At 2.2 miles the trail begins to level out. There are some small rock spurs on the right and a good spot for camping close to the rocks, which provide a panoramic view into the Saint Marys. The trail begins a series of easy ups and downs near the crest of Cellar Mountain among many low shrubs of mountain laurel and rhododendron. Teaberry also grows here, and tree species include oak, maple, hickory, and a few unusual species such as table mountain pine and chinquapin.

The trail begins an easy descent to a saddle about 2.8 miles from the trailhead. Past the saddle, the Cellar Mountain Trail begins an easy climb to a jeep road. Take a left on the jeep road and walk about 100 yards to the trailhead for the Cold Springs Trail, about 3.2 miles into the hike.

The Cold Springs Trail descends 2.1 miles to FR 42. Begin a steep descent on a narrow path crowded with mountain laurel and small pine and oak. The steep ridge drops away from the trail quickly. About 0.7 mile from the junction a large rock outcrop affords a good view of the upper Shenandoah Valley and the mountains to the west. The trail then makes a wide left U-turn and begins to drop toward the creek. There is one switchback during the descent. After crossing a rock river, the grade moderates and the hiking becomes much easier.

A small pond is reached about 1.5 miles from the junction. An old rock retaining wall acts as a dam. The pool is a pleasant spot to have a snack and filter some water for the return trip to the parking area. After leaving the pond, the trail passes through a wet region. There is a large amount of undergrowth, so off-trail travel to avoid the water is limited. The wide, easy-to-follow trail exits the wilderness and intersects with FR 42. Turn left on this road and walk 1.8 miles back to the Cellar Mountain Trailhead and parking area.

Overnight Backpack

Saint Marys/Mine Bank Trail Loop

Distance: 15.1 miles.
Difficulty: Strenuous.
Topo maps: Vesuvius-VA and Big Levels-VA.

HOW TO GET THERE: Take Interstate 81 to exit 205, south of Staunton. Turn east on County Road 606. At the T intersection, turn left on US 11, proceed 100 yards, and turn right on Virginia Highway 56. Travel 1.2 miles, cross the South River, and turn left on CR 608. Drive 2.2 miles to a yield sign. Turn right under the train trestle and continue on CR 608. Travel 0.3 mile to FR 41 (St. Marys Road) and turn right. Continue 1.4 miles to the Saint Marys Trail parking area.

The Saint Marys Trail is a wonderful trail that slowly climbs up to Green Pond, a small natural pond located in Big Levels. Marked with blue blazes, the trail begins at an elevation of approximately 1,700 feet and is generally an easy hike, with the exception of the creek crossings and the steep climb to Green Pond. There is a Forest Service information center at the parking lot; just beyond is a livestock fence. The clear, rushing Saint Marys River is on the right, in a forest of tulip poplar, hemlock, oak, and black cherry. A small spring crosses the creek, where there is evidence of some beaver activity. There are also signs of the past mining operations that dominated the region in the early 1900s. The valley is a narrow steep-walled gorge with many rock rivers and small cliffs. Numerous campsites dot the trail's edges.

If the water is high at the first creek crossing, the only way to cross is in bare feet. The trail narrows shortly after this crossing. Erosion is actively cutting away the right bank; footing can be treacherous in this area. At 1.4 miles, the Saint Marys Falls Trail makes a short 0.5-mile trip up the Saint Marys River to the falls, requiring two creek crossings.

From the junction with the Saint Marys Falls Trail, the Saint Marys Trail turns southwest and enters the Sugar Tree Branch. The trail narrows as it moves up the hollow among large tulip poplars and hemlocks. At a small clearing, about 0.4 mile from the trail junction, cross the creek and turn left. Upon entering a canyon, the trail climbs sharply and then enters an old mining site. Follow the trail to the back of the old settling pond and then out of the clearing into the woods, where the ground is covered with blueberry, huckleberry, and teaberry. The trail meanders in and out of small hollows to the intersection with the Mine Bank Trail 3.7 miles from the trailhead. The elevation at the trail junction is 2,200 feet.

Beyond the Mine Bank Trail, the Saint Marys Trail is fairly level. At 4.7 miles it crosses the Bear Branch twice. A bushwhack up the Bear Branch leads to some nice falls. After the second crossing, there are again ruins of an old mining camp. From here, the Saint Marys River quickly loses its strength. After several creek crossings, the river is left behind and the trail climbs rapidly to the Big Levels and Green Pond. The trail leaves the wilderness, entering the Green Pond area approximately 6 miles from the trailhead. Sedge and cranberry thrive around the pond.

The Saint Marys Trail intersects with a jeep trail (FR 162) about 0.3 mile beyond Green Pond. Turn right on the jeep trail and walk approximately 2.8 miles to a fork in the road. The left fork leads to the Blue Ridge Parkway near milepost 22. Take the right fork and walk approximately 0.4 mile to the 1.8-mile Bald Mountain Trail, which exits the jeep road to the right. The Bald Mountain Trail begins with a long descent to a small creek, then crosses two creeks and intersects with a road that leads down the Bear Branch. Follow the Bald Mountain Trail as it meanders along the mountainside, following an easy grade. The trail crosses three more small creeks and then follows an old road. After crossing an earthen barrier, the Bald Mountain Trail intersects with the Mine Bank Trail.

The Mine Bank Trailhead is located near milepost 23 on the Blue Ridge Parkway at the Fork Mountain Overlook. This 3-mile trail begins with an easy grade that soon becomes steep. After entering a narrow valley, the trail begins to parallel the noisy little Mine Bank Creek. At about 1.3 miles, cross the creek at the top of a 15-foot section of small falls.

The trail continues to descend, crossing the creek several times. About 1.8 miles from the Bald Mountain Trail, rock outcroppings line both sides of the trail. These outcrops are a familiar sight in the Saint Marys Wilderness and are an integral part of what makes this area unique. After another 0.2 mile, the stream falls away sharply to the right. Another set of falls can be heard, but it is difficult to get a clear view of them. To view the falls more clearly, walk a short distance beyond them, then walk carefully down to the creek bed. Look upstream for an unobstructed view of the falls.

Just before the intersection with the Saint Marys Trail, the Mine Bank Trail climbs a small finger ridge and then begins to drop again. At the intersection with the Saint Marys Trail, turn left to head back to the trailhead.

Day Trip

Big Spy Mountain

Distance: 3.0 miles round-trip.
Difficulty: Easy.
Topo maps: Vesuvius-VA and Big Levels-VA.

HOW TO GET THERE: Take the Blue Ridge Parkway to a small parking area on the west side of the parkway between mileposts 25 and 26. There are two Forest Service gates at the parking area; do not block them.

Signs indicate that the beginning of this trail is on private property. To avoid the posted property, travel about 100 yards downhill from the parking lot, then contour along the mountain to the south about 150 yards to an old road. This bypass is a short bushwhack.

At the old road, turn right (west) and travel downhill, crossing a saddle before beginning the climb up Big Spy Mountain. The trail is at times difficult to see, so be alert for changes in its direction. The climb is marked by short steep sections followed by easy breathers. Four large boulders mark the gateway to the top; just beyond is the end of Big Spy Mountain Trail and a rock outcrop that affords an excellent view to the south and west. A tremendous boulder field that leads down to the North Fork of Spy Run is an interesting area to explore if time permits.

Adams Peak Roadless Area

Location: 12 miles northeast of Lexington, Virginia.
Size: 7,076 acres.
Administration: USDAFS George Washington National Forest, Pedlar Ranger District.
Management status: Nonwilderness roadless area.
Ecosystems: Eastern deciduous forest.
Elevation range: 1,200 to 3,200 feet.
System trails: 11 miles.
Maximum core-to-perimeter distance: 2.5 miles. (Note: Although technically the farthest distance from the middle of the trail to the perimeter is 5.5 miles along the trail, if injured or lost the best course of action is to leave the trail and follow the side of the mountain down to the road for a maximum distance of 2.5 miles.)
Activities: Hiking, horseback riding, and hunting.
Modes of travel: Foot and horse.
Maps: Pedlar Ranger District map; Cornwall-VA, Montebello-VA, and Vesuvius-VA 1:24,000 topo maps.

OVERVIEW: Adams Peak is located on the western side of the Blue Ridge Mountains in a region known as the Blue Ridge Complex, which contains Cambrian volcanic and sedimentary rock. Three major mountains dominate the western face of the roadless area. At 3,060 feet, South Mountain is the tallest. Steep, rugged slopes characterize the area around Adams Peak, a huge, tree-covered mound to the north of South Mountain. Completing the triumvirate is McClung Mountain. The eastern sides of these three mountains are joined together by Whetstone Ridge.

Where Whetstone Ridge and the three mountains join, two bowls with narrow outlets are formed: Dismal Hollow is formed by Whetstone Ridge and Adams Peak; Taylor Hollow lies between Adams Peak and McClung Mountain. The major watersheds on the east side of the ridge are Dark Hollow, Big Dark Hollow, and Big Bend Creek. Big Marys Creek is the only major stream within the roadless area. Backcountry visitors should pack in plenty of water.

Several holes dug in the ground, the only evidence of past mining activity, are visible near the summit of South Mountain. Besides these old scars, little else disturbs the rugged, scenic beauty.

RECREATIONAL USES: Hiking and hunting are the two major activities in the Adams Peak Roadless Area. Most of the hiking within the roadless area takes

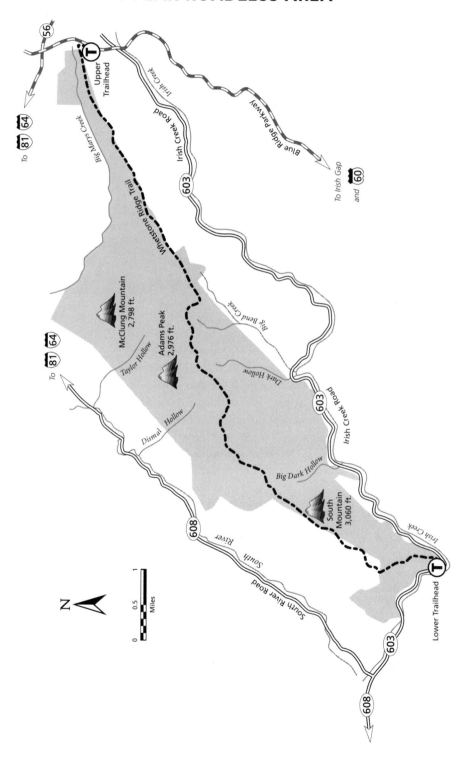

An old sign on the Whetstone Ridge Trail.

place along the Whetstone Ridge Trail. This 11-mile trail climbs from Irish Creek to the crest of the Blue Ridge. This trail is usually free of windfall and is suitable for horseback riding. The parking lots at each end of the trail are large enough to accommodate a horse trailer. Most of the rest of the region is inaccessible because of steep slopes and laurel thickets. Roads along the boundaries provide hunter access to the outer fringe of this wild area.

Shuttle Day Hike

Whetstone Ridge Trail

Distance: 11 miles one way.
Difficulty: Moderate or strenuous, depending on the hiking direction.
Topo maps: Cornwall-VA, Montbello-VA, and Vesuvius-VA.

HOW TO GET THERE: *Upper trailhead*—From the junction of Virginia Highway 56 and the Blue Ridge Parkway, drive 2.4 miles south on the Blue Ridge Parkway to milepost 29. The Whetstone Ridge Store is on the west side of the parkway. The trailhead is located at the parking lot.

Lower trailhead—From the junction of Interstates 81 and 64 near Lexington, take I–64 west. Take exit 55, turn south on US 11, and travel 0.9 mile to a stoplight just before the bridge. Turn left at the stoplight and travel 3.8 miles to a stop sign. Turn right and go 0.4 mile to a left turn onto South River Road. Travel 3.8 miles to Irish Creek Road, turn right, and continue 2.3 miles to a parking lot on the right. The trailhead is on the left side on the road.

The Whetstone Ridge Trail is best done with a car shuttle or as an overnight backpack trip. This trail description begins from the lower trailhead on Irish Creek Road. The well-maintained trail, marked with yellow blazes, climbs from the Irish Creek valley to the crest of Blue Ridge Mountain, gaining 1,900 feet along the way.

After crossing the road, the trail begins by climbing the ridge. A sign indicates distances to South Mountain (3 miles) and the Blue Ridge Parkway (11 miles). At 0.1 mile the path joins an old road, and at 1.3 miles intersects with another road climbing up the ridge. A sign reads OLD TRAM ROAD and WHETSTONE RIDGE TRAIL. At 1.8 miles the trail crests the ridge and passes through a region of sinkholes, remnants of past mining activity.

The trail reaches the summit of South Mountain (elevation 3,060 feet), and then descends. After contouring along the eastern side of the mountain, the trail wraps around the end of a huge bowl. About halfway around the bowl, a sign marks a short trail on the left, which leads to a small rock outcrop. There is an excellent view from here of the steep-walled bowl and of Adams Peak. Not far from this first view sign, another sign marks a rock outcrop with a view of the Blue Ridge Mountains and Irish Creek watershed.

The Whetstone Ridge Trail continues along the ridge in a series of gentle ups and downs. After passing under a power line, the trail leaves national forest land and enters land managed by the National Park Service. The trail descends some stairs and passes a sign for the Whetstone Ridge Trail with distances to South Mountain (8 miles) and County Road 603 (11 miles). The trail ends at the parking lot on the Blue Ridge Parkway.

Mount Pleasant National Scenic Area ▮ 11

Location: 11 miles east of Buena Vista, Virginia.
Size: 7,580 acres.
Administration: USDAFS George Washington National Forest, Pedlar Ranger District.
Management status: National scenic area.
Ecosystems: Eastern deciduous forest.
Elevation range: 1,400 to 4,071 feet.
System trails: 13.5 miles.
Maximum core-to-perimeter distance: 2.5 miles.
Activities: Hiking, backpacking, rock climbing, bouldering, and fishing.
Modes of travel: Foot and horse.
Maps: Pedlar Ranger District map; Forks of Buffalo-VA and Montbello-VA 1:24,000 topo maps.

OVERVIEW: Mount Pleasant National Scenic Area is a high region along the Blue Ridge Mountains. The area is marked by steep rugged terrain with gentle rounded summits. Within the boundaries of the Scenic Area are four peaks slightly above 4,000 feet, each offering unique natural beauty. Cole Mountain is a high meadow with a panoramic view of the Scenic Area. Mount Pleasant's rocky summit offers a tremendous view of the piedmont and is home to a thriving community of mountain ash and yellow birch. Mount Pompey's tree-covered summit is a stark contrast to the summits of both Mount Pleasant and Cole Mountain. Bald Knob, contrary to its name, is no longer bald, but one can see firsthand the process of change from one type of ecosystem to another.

The watersheds of this rugged area are generally V-shaped, with swift running streams. The major creeks of the Mount Pleasant area include Cove Creek, Little Cove Creek, and Rocky Branch, all of which flow into the Buffalo River. Indian Creek flows into the Tye River.

The sheltered coves provide habitat for several species of cove hardwoods, some of which are considered old-growth forest. Red oak, scarlet oak, and chestnut oak dominate the drier ridges on the eastern slopes. Pitch pine and Virginia pine are also found in these areas.

RECREATIONAL USES: Hiking is one of the major recreational activities in the Mount Pleasant National Scenic Area. Two great loop trails, the Harry B. Lanum Trail and the Hotel Trail/AT Loop provide easy day hikes for almost

Views

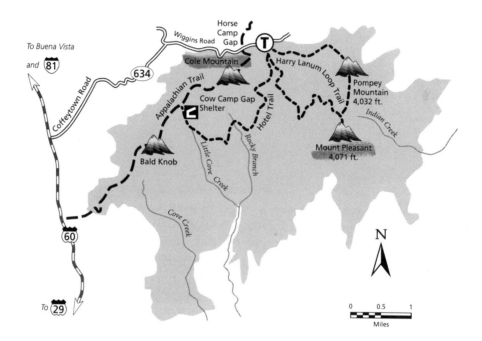

any ability. The Harry B. Lanum Loop sports one major climb and several great views. The Hotel Trail has two major climbs, but the views are worth the effort. The two loops have a common trailhead and can be combined into one long, moderately strenuous loop. The AT shelter near Cow Camp Gap can be utilized for an easy overnight trip.

The meadow on the summit of Cole Mountain and the mountain-ash-covered summit of Mount Pleasant provide some of the best scenery in the Pedlar District of the George Washington National Forest. Many photographs have been taken on these lofty summits, and there's even some excitement for history buffs: A Civil War–era stone fence built up the southern ridge of Cole Mountain.

Day Hike

Harry Lanum Loop Trail

Distance: 5.2 miles.
Difficulty: Easy.
Topo map: Forks of Buffalo-VA and Montebello-VA.

HOW TO GET THERE: *From Lexington,* take Interstate 81 to exit 188 and turn east on US 60. Travel 12.4 miles to Coffeytown Road, County Road 634. Turn left onto CR 634 and proceed 1.7 miles to Wiggins Road; bear right at the Y in the road. Travel 3.0 miles (go past the parking area for the Appalachian Trail) and turn right at the sign for the Mount Pleasant National Scenic Area Hiking Trail. Travel 0.1 mile to the parking area.

From Lynchburg, take US 29 north to US 60. Turn west on US 60 and drive 18.4 miles to Coffeytown Road, CR 634. Turn right onto CR 634 and follow the directions above.

There is a Forest Service information center at the beginning of the trail. To hike the loop in a counterclockwise direction, take the trail that exits the parking area to the left. After crossing a gate, the trail begins a long, easy descent, and crosses three small creeks. The trail actually follows an old railroad grade through an area composed mainly of small second-growth hardwoods. When the trail begins to climb toward the saddle between Mount Pleasant and Pompey Mountain, watch the trail markers closely because the trail makes a sudden left turn off the old railroad grade, which continues straight. Near this point is an immense black cherry tree.

The trail becomes a steep path, and large boulders dot the landscape. Upon reaching the saddle, the region is flat. At a Y intersection, take the right fork, which leads to Mount Pleasant and a 0.5-mile spur trail to the summit. The left fork is a shortcut to another section of the Harry Lanum Trail close to Pompey Mountain.

The spur exits to the right and begins with a moderate climb, becoming easy near the summit crest. Once on the crest, the trail forks to the right and left. The right fork leads to a rock outcrop with a good view of the Blue Ridge Mountain to the north and south. Bald Mountain and the grassy summit of Cole Mountain are visible in the foreground. The slope of the ridge is covered with mountain ash, which produce brilliant red berries in the fall. The left fork leads to a rock outcrop on the east end of the mountain, and a grassy campsite. There is an excellent view of the piedmont.

To continue the loop, turn left at the junction with the summit spur and walk toward Pompey Mountain. The trail climbs gradually toward the summit. After a short distance, there is a trail to the left and a sign that lists the distance to Pompey Mountain as 0.8 mile. On the right side of the trail are several large rocks. Near the summit of Pompey Mountain is another Y junction; bear to the left. Just past this junction, a steep descent of approximately 0.5 mile is followed by an easier grade. The trail ends at an earthen barrier and a livestock gate.

Day Hike

Hotel Trail/Appalachian Trail Loop

Distance: 6.2 miles.
Difficulty: Moderate.
Topo map: Forks of Buffalo-VA and Montebello-VA.

HOW TO GET THERE: Follow the directions to the trailhead for the Harry Lanum Loop Trail.

The signed trailhead for the blue blazed Hotel Trail is located on the right side of the parking area. After passing through a brier thicket and a livestock gate, a sign gives distances to Cow Camp Gap Shelter (3.0 miles) and the AT (3.5 miles). The trail follows an old road and begins with an easy descent that is followed by an easy climb. When the Hotel Trail breaks into a clearing, there is a good view of both Pompey Mountain and Mount Pleasant, as well as a sign for water and a small spring on the left.

Past the spring, the trail leaves the road and enters the woods for a short distance, then comes back to the road and enters a large field on the shoulder of the mountain. A large well-shaped oak tree at the end of the meadow marks an excellent camping spot. At the tree, the trail bends right and begins to descend as the trail narrows and passes through a thicket of pine. The trail crosses a dry creek bed, then reaches an old stone fence, built in the 1850s, that climbs up

A view to the west from Cole Mountain.

the side of the mountain. For the next 0.75 mile, the trail meanders along the side of the mountain, slowly gaining elevation. After cresting a finger ridge, there is a difficult 0.25 mile descent to the Cow Camp Gap Shelter, where you'll find a picnic table and privy.

Past the shelter, climb 0.5 mile to the AT, passing through a forest of knurled oak and storm-damaged trees. Two trees of note in this area are black cherry and yellow birch. At the intersection with the AT, a sign gives the distance to US 60 (3.8 miles) and Horse Camp Gap (2.8 miles).

Turning right, the white blazed AT begins a steep, difficult climb straight up the ridge. At the ridge top, the grade moderates quickly and the walking is much easier. The AT passes through the remains of an old stone fence before climbing into the meadow on Cole Mountain (elevation 4,022 feet), where the view is spectacular. The AT descends through the meadow to a gravel road that leads into the woods. About 100 yards after entering the woods, the AT turns left and exits the road. The descent to Horse Camp Gap is moderate and punctuated by several turns, and is at times rocky. At the intersection with Wiggins Road (FR 51), turn right and return 0.4 mile to the parking area.

Three Sisters Roadless Area

Location: 10 miles south of Lexington, Virginia.
Size: 8,150 acres.
Administration: USDAFS George Washington National Forest, Pedlar Ranger District.
Management status: Nonwilderness roadless area.
Ecosystems: Eastern deciduous forest.
Elevation range: 900 to 2,992 feet.
System trails: 8 miles.
Maximum core-to-perimeter distance: 1.75 miles.
Activities: Hiking.
Modes of travel: Foot.
Maps: Pedlar Ranger District map; Buena Vista-VA, Glasgow-VA, and Snowden-VA 1:24,000 topo maps.

OVERVIEW: The Three Sisters region is a rugged mountain area dominated by three knobs that overlook the town of Glasgow. These knobs are the high western shoulders of the ridge climbing to the summit of Bluff Mountain. Steep rugged slopes characterize the Three Sisters region. Another rocky knob, the Pinnacle, lies to the northeast of the Three Sisters Knobs. There are many rock rivers on the side of these knobs. The eastern side of the ridge, remarkably different from the western ridge, climbs rapidly from the James River and culminates with a rocky ledge known as Rocky Row. The long ridge of Rocky Row runs almost the entire length of the roadless area. Beginning near US 501, this ridge climbs almost to the summit of Bluff Mountain, which is located just outside the roadless area boundary.

Pitch pine, Virginia pine, and chestnut oak dominate much of the western slopes. Several species of oak and hickory make up the overstory along the ridge crest. Near the summit of Bluff Mountain, just outside the roadless boundary, a small stand of red spruce was planted to help locate an old fire tower. The upper Belle Cove watershed supports a thriving stand of cove hardwoods.

Belle Cove Branch, Bennetts Run, and Davidson Run drain the west regions of the Three Sisters. Bennetts Run has a small population of native brook trout. Johns Hollow, Cedar Branch Hollow, and Grants Hollow drain the southeastern section. The headwaters of Otter Creek are located near Saltlog Gap. Despite all these streams, there is little water available along the trails within the area's boundary.

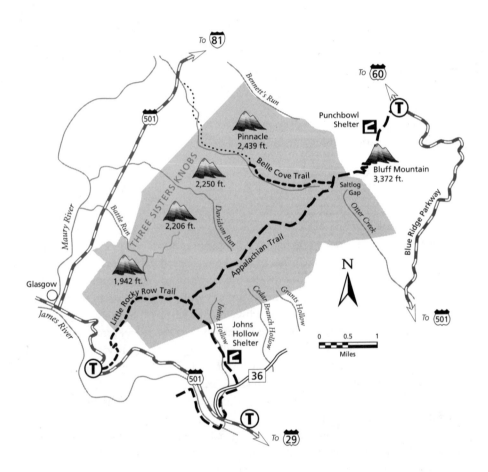

RECREATIONAL USES: Hiking and hunting are the major recreational activities of the Three Sisters, as well as camping and backpacking. The Appalachian Trail, the premier trail through the region, begins near the bridge at Snowden and makes a tough climb to Rocky Row. From there it continues climbing to the summit of Bluff Mountain. The well-maintained Little Rocky Row Trail offers a shorter and easy climb to the scenic views on Rocky Row. The Belle Cove Trail is the third major trail into this roadless area. Unfortunately, the lower portions of the trail were wiped out during the torrential rains in 1995. The lower portion of the Belle Cove Trail is now a bushwhack, and provides ample opportunity to view the scouring forces of water and stone.

Bear hunting is popular in the Three Sisters area. The more rugged areas support a small but thriving bear population. Many roads lead to the fringes of the Three Sisters, allowing easy access into even some of the more remote sections on the eastern side of the ridge. There is a small brook trout population in Bennetts Creek, but access to National Forest land is difficult because of private landholdings on both sides of the creek leading into the forest.

Day Hike

Little Rocky Row Trail

Distance: 6.0 miles round-trip.
Difficulty: Moderate.
Topo map: Glasgow-VA and Snowden-VA.

HOW TO GET THERE: *From Lexington,* take Interstate 81 south to exit 180. Turn south on US 11 and proceed 4.4 miles to the intersection of US 11 and Virginia Highway 130. Turn left on VA 130 and travel 6.4 miles to the intersection of VA 130 and US 501. Turn right on US 501/VA 130 and travel 2.5 miles to the top of the mountain. The parking area for the Little Rocky Row Trail is on the right.

From Lynchburg, take US 29 to VA 130, turn west on VA 130 and proceed 24.1 miles to the Little Rocky Row parking area on the left at the top of the mountain.

The Little Rocky Row Trail climbs 1,250 feet from US 501 to the intersection with the Appalachian Trail. From the parking area, hike west on US 501 about 100 yards. The trailhead is located on the right side of the road. A marker about 0.1 mile from the trailhead gives the distances to the AT (3 miles) and Bluff Mountain (8 miles).

The trail climbs to a power line and then becomes very steep. Five switchbacks aid in the short climb to the ridge. Once on the crest, the grade is much easier. The trail continues on or near the crest for the remainder of the hike.

A white-tailed deer on Rocky Row.

Huckleberry and blueberry line the trail along the crest. Their berries make a tasty snack for hikers in August. About 2 miles from the trailhead, the Little Rocky Row Trail crests a knoll and begins to descend. The trail is rocky, and there is a good view to the west after the leaves have fallen.

Shortly after crossing a saddle, the Little Rocky Row Trail intersects with the Appalachian Trail. A sign at the junction gives distances to the Punchbowl Shelter (6.7 miles north) and the Johns Hollow Shelter (2.1 miles south). Continue up the ridge on the AT about 200 yards to a rock outcrop from which there is a good view of the James River Face Wilderness. Retrace your route to the trailhead.

Day Hike or Overnighter

Appalachian Trail

Distance: 11.8 miles one way.
Difficulty: Easy.
Topo map: Buena Vista-VA, Glasgow-VA, and Snowden-VA.

HOW TO GET THERE: *Beginning trailhead*—From Lexington, follow the preceding directions to the Rocky Row Trailhead. Continue 3.6 miles to the AT parking area on the right.

From Lynchburg, take US 29 north to Virginia Highway 130. Turn west on VA 130 and proceed 20.2 miles to the AT parking area on the left.

Ending trailhead—At the intersection of VA 130 and the Blue Ridge Parkway, travel south on the Parkway to a small parking area on the right. The parking area is between milepost 51 and 52.

This section of the AT begins by paralleling US 501 a short distance. The trail crosses US 501 and follows Hercules Road approximately 50 feet before exiting into the woods on the right. There is a quick drop down Rocky Row Run, then the AT crosses the run via a bridge. A short climb is followed by a short gradual descent back to Rocky Row Run, which is crossed a second time via a bridge.

The trail makes a short climb to an old road, then follows the road approximately 0.3 mile on an easy grade. Just before reaching a gravel road, there is a left switchback and the trail begins a moderate climb to FR 36. After crossing FR 36, a sign marks the distance to Johns Hollow Shelter (0.6 mile). The trail climbs a finger ridge before dropping down to and crossing a small creek.

At approximately 2 miles, a blue blazed trail exits to the right. This leads to Johns Hollow Shelter, a short hike from the AT, where water is available. Continue north on the AT another 2.1 miles to the junction with the Little Rocky

Looking east from Rocky Row.

Row Trail. On the ridge crest is a rock outcrop with a great view. A car shuttle between the trailheads for this section of the AT and the Little Rocky Row Trail creates a day hike of approximately 7.6 miles.

Continue climbing 5 miles on the AT along the Rocky Row Ridge to the summit of Bluff Mountain. Continue north to Punchbowl Shelter, which has a spring, table, and privy. The shelter is 6.7 miles from the junction with the Little Rocky Row Trail. Hike another 0.5 mile north to the Blue Ridge Parkway parking area.

Barbours Creek Wilderness 13

Location: 22 miles north of Roanoke, Virginia.
Size: 6,432 acres.
Administration: USDAFS Jefferson National Forest, New Castle District.
Management status: 5,700-acre wilderness and 732-acre nonwilderness roadless area.
Ecosystems: Eastern deciduous forest.
Elevation range: 1,612 to 3,804 feet.
System trails: 12.8 miles.
Maximum core-to-perimeter distance: 1.5 miles.
Activities: Hiking, hunting, and fishing.
Modes of travel: Foot and horse.
Maps: New Castle District map; New Castle-VA, Jordan Mines-VA, and Potts Creek-VA and WVA 1:24,000 topo map.

OVERVIEW: Barbours Creek was declared a wilderness area in 1987. The wilderness is located on the eastern side of Potts Mountain, and the mountain crest forms the western boundary of the roadless area. Barbours Creek marks the eastern boundary of the wilderness. Gradually sloping from the creek to Potts Mountain, the landscape grows very steep and rugged near the crest.

Nearly 20 miles of trails thread through the wilderness, roadless area, and surrounding forest lands, but Lipes Branch Trail is the only maintained trail within the designated wilderness. All the other trails follow old roads in various states of decay. Water is available in most regions of the wilderness, with the exception of the crest of Potts Mountain, where it is scarce. The area sees little visitation except during hunting season. The avid backwoods hiker can find plenty of solitude here.

There are several interesting areas in the Barbours Creek Wilderness. A large bald lies just outside the western boundary on the top of Potts Mountain. The bald comprises approximately 50 acres and affords a spectacular view. The region around Forest Road 176 is an easy-to-reach rock formation. The rocks are spread pell-mell throughout a small creek bed and provide some fun scrambling.

RECREATIONAL USES: Hiking is the major recreational activity in the Barbours Creek Wilderness. There is only one maintained trail in the wilderness; however, there are several old roads that provide excellent access into the lower regions of the Barbours Creek area. The Potts Mountain Jeep Trail that forms

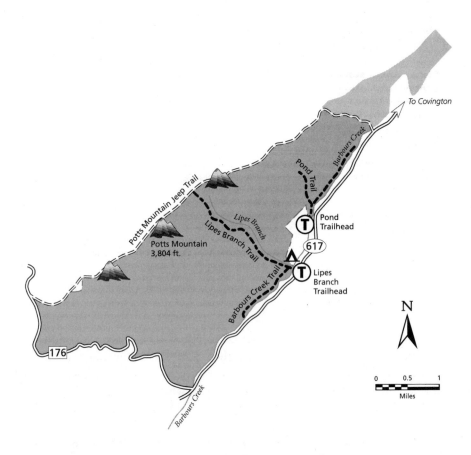

To Covington

Barbours Creek

Potts Mountain Jeep Trail

Pond Trail

Lipes Branch

Lipes Branch Trail

Potts Mountain
3,804 ft.

Pond
Trailhead

617

Lipes
Branch
Trailhead

Barbours Creek Trail

176

Barbours Creek

N

0   0.5   1
Miles

An old fire road marks the boundary of Barbours Creek Wilderness at the crest of Potts Mountain.

the western boundary of the wilderness provides access to the upper end of the Lipes Branch Trail as well as other upper areas of the region. Hunters are found in great numbers during the open firearm season; it is best to avoid this area during hunting season. Finally, anglers will find plenty of excitement on Barbours Creek.

Day Hike

Lipes Branch Trail

Distance: 4 miles round-trip.
Difficulty: Moderate.
Topo map: New Castle-VA.

HOW TO GET THERE: From Interstate 64 at Covington, take exit 21 and turn left at the stop sign onto County Road 696. Drive 0.2 mile and turn right onto CR 616. Go 5.5 miles south to a T intersection, turn right to stay on CR 616, and continue 6.8 miles. Turn left on CR 617 and continue 7.2 miles south to the Lipes Branch parking lot and trailhead on the right just past the campground.

Lipes Branch Trail climbs from the base of Potts Mountain to the crest. The yellow blazed trail begins at the Forest Service information center. After 0.1 mile a trail splits to the left and traces an old road south along Barbours Creek; stay straight on Lipes Branch Trail. At 0.2 mile a spur trail forks right to Lipes Branch Campground. The forest here is composed of tall cove hardwoods such as red oak, white oak, and tulip poplar.

About 0.6 mile the trailhead, the grade becomes moderate. The path begins a steady ascent up a shoulder of Potts Mountain. Here mountain laurel, pine, and chestnut oak are the dominant trees. Soon the trail crosses a dry creek bed and becomes steep. Two switchbacks mark the start of the final ascent to a small clearing at the top of Potts Mountain. At the summit, the Lipes Branch Trail joins the Potts Mountain Jeep Trail, marked by a small sign. A short walk north on the jeep road leads to a larger clearing with excellent views to the east and west. For the return trip, follow your route back to the trailhead.

Day Hike

Barbours Creek Trail

Distance: 2.6 miles round-trip.
Difficulty: Easy.
Topo map: New Castle-VA.

HOW TO GET THERE: Follow the preceding directions to the Lipes Branch Trailhead.

This hike follows a scenic trail along Barbours Creek. From the Lipes Branch Trailhead, walk about 50 yards west on Lipes Branch Trail to a small clearing, where Barbours Creek Trail goes left on an old road. There is no trail sign, but the junction is obvious.

The trail enters a stand of small hardwoods. These trees abruptly give way to huge cove hardwoods that are tall, straight, and beautiful. From here, the trail meanders through several small clearings to meet with Barbours Creek. To continue, you must ford the creek, which can be difficult when the water is high. If you want to return on the same trail, don't bother crossing the creek; just retrace your steps to the trailhead. The other option here is to ford the creek and continue south about 0.1 mile to join County Road 617. Turn left and walk about 1.2 miles north on CR 617 to return to the trailhead.

Day Hike

Pond Trail

Distance: 2.2 miles round-trip.
Difficulty: Easy.
Topo maps: New Castle-VA and Jordan Mines-VA.

HOW TO GET THERE: Follow the Lipes Branch Trail directions to County Road 617. Drive 5.9 miles south on CR 617 to a small road on the right. This turn is easy to miss; if you reach the campground, you've gone too far south. Turn onto the small road and park in the clearing.

The parking area for this trail is located 1.3 miles north of the Lipes Branch Trail parking lot and trailhead. If you're looking for an out-of-the-way place to camp, this trail fills the bill. From the parking lot, an old road crosses the creek and then parallels it for a short distance. Near a dry creek bed, the trail turns left and quickly climbs the mountain, following a narrow ravine. The forest is composed primarily of oak, maple, and hickory.

At 0.8 mile, the trail enters a small clearing and then leaves on the far side through a small pine grove. Just beyond the pines, there is a small man-made pond. The trail continues past the pond, but dead-ends a short distance later.

Shawvers Run Wilderness

Location: 22 miles northwest of Roanoke, Virginia.
Size: 6,640 acres.
Administration: USDAFS Jefferson National Forest, New Castle District.
Management status: 3,570-acre wilderness and 3,070-acre nonwilderness roadless area.
Ecosystems: Eastern deciduous forest.
Elevation range: 1,960 to 3,800 feet.
System trails: 4.7 miles of trail and old roads.
Maximum core-to-perimeter distance: 1.3 miles.
Activities: Hiking, hunting, and fishing.
Modes of travel: Foot.
Maps: New Castle District map; Paint Bank-VA and WVA, and Potts Creek-VA and WVA 1:24,000 topo maps.

OVERVIEW: Shawvers Run is a small wilderness located in the New Castle District of Jefferson National Forest. Encompassing about 3,570 acres, the area was designated a wilderness by Congress in 1987.

Shawvers Run Wilderness includes a long spur on the western side of Potts Mountain. This spur separates the drainage basins for the two major creeks in the region. Shawvers Run drains the northeastern area of the wilderness, while Valley Branch drains the southwestern portion. Even though both of these creeks are small, water does flow year-round.

Three interesting features within the wilderness are worth visiting. The first is a narrow canyon that carries Valley Branch. This sheltered canyon is covered with lush green foliage and is very remote. The second feature is Hanging Rock, an outcrop overlooking Hanging Rock Valley. On clear days it is possible to see the Blue Ridge Mountains in the east and West Virginia to the west. The third landmark is the saddle between Shawvers Run and Valley Branch. A clearing marks the end of the high spot in the middle of this wilderness, and just below the ridge top is an impact crater from a fighter jet that crashed there in 1993.

Forest composition varies throughout the wilderness. The Valley Branch drainage supports cove hardwoods such as poplar and birch, as well as evergreens like hemlock and white pine. These woods are in stark contrast to the dry, exposed spur west of Potts Mountain. Here, Virginia pine and chestnut oak dominate the overstory. Much of the remainder of the landscape is clothed

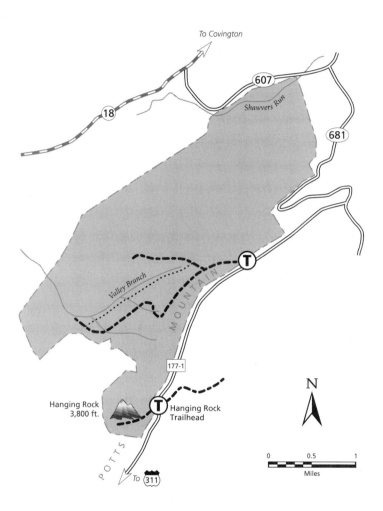

in oak-hickory forest common throughout Virginia's mountains. Also scattered throughout the area are dogwood, striped maple, rhododendron, mountain laurel, and serviceberry.

RECREATIONAL USES: The wilderness is completely undeveloped and has no existing maintained trail system, but several old roads pierce the wilderness. These roads provide fairly easy access into the heart of Shawvers Run. Along with some short cross-country hikes, the roads provide 4.7 miles of hiking for the avid backwoods hiker. The area is seldom visited, except during hunting season, and thus it provides plenty of quiet, undisturbed hiking.

Day Hike

Hanging Rock Trail

Distance: 0.8 mile round-trip.
Difficulty: Easy.
Topo map: Potts Creek-VA and WVA.

HOW TO GET THERE: From Interstate 64 in Covington, take exit 16 and turn right at the stop sign. At the next stoplight, turn left. Drive 1 mile and turn left at the stoplight onto Virginia Highway 18. Drive 20.6 miles southwest on VA 18 and turn left onto County Road 607. Go 1.4 miles east and turn right on CR 681. Drive 3.3 miles south to the top of Potts Mountain. Turn right on Forest Road 177-1 and continue 3.4 miles south to a small parking lot on the right.

The trail begins with an easy climb through mixed hardwoods and rhododendron, winding southwest toward Hanging Rock. Although not marked, the trail's direction is clear. When the path begins to descend, small rock outcroppings are visible on the left. Just beyond these small rock cliffs is Hanging Rock, which provides a spectacular view. To the northwest is Shawvers Run Wilderness. The long ridge to the southeast is Potts Mountain; the ridge to the west is Peters Mountain. Hanging Rock Valley lies between the two mountains. After enjoying the view, retrace your route to the trailhead.

Day Hike

Valley Branch Trail/Bushwhack

Distance: 4.2-mile loop.
Difficulty: Moderate.
Topo map: Potts Creek-VA and WVA.

Rhododendron bloom throughout Virginia in the spring.

HOW TO GET THERE: From Interstate 64 in Covington, take exit 16 and turn right at the stop sign. At the next stoplight, turn left. Drive 1 mile and turn left at the stoplight onto Virginia Highway 18. Drive 20.6 miles southwest on VA 18 and turn left onto County Road 607. Go 1.4 miles east and turn right on CR 681. Drive 3.3 miles south to the top of Potts Mountain. Turn right on Forest Road 177-1 and continue 1.6 miles south to a small parking lot on the right.

The trailhead is marked by large boulders and a small wilderness sign. The trail follows an old road from the top of Potts Mountain to the Valley Branch. The road is in good condition and hiking is easy. At 0.8 mile, cross the first of three small springs. Thickets of small hardwoods crowd the trail on both sides. After crossing the third creek, there is a small clearing, a good location for some "off the beaten path" camping.

Past the clearing the trees become much taller. Large tulip poplar, oak, and hickory line the trail all the way to the Valley Branch. At 1.5 miles, the trail bends right and drops steeply to the end of the road. At this point the trail makes a sharp left turn and becomes a footpath. After about 1 mile the path starts paralleling the wilderness boundary. In a clearing at 2.2 miles there is a hunting cabin that belongs to an organization called the Pond Hunting Club.

Continue 0.4 mile downhill into the Valley Branch basin. This is an easy bushwhack. Follow the small creek to the narrow ravine. This area is home to many tall hemlock, white pine, and rhododendron thickets. This region is exceptionally beautiful and worth the extra effort you'll make reaching it.

To return to the trailhead, follow the old road that parallels Valley Branch upstream, leading up the creek to a small clearing. At times this old road is barely visible and might be hard to follow. It climbs to within 0.5 mile of the saddle between Valley Branch and Shawvers Run. The last 0.5 mile is a definite bushwhack. Keep aiming uphill and north. Once on the saddle, turn right and follow the saddle back to the old road that leads down to the Valley Branch. Turn left on this road to return to the trailhead.

Mountain Lake Wilderness

Location: 13 miles north of Blacksburg, Virginia.
Size: 16,729 acres.
Administration: USDAFS Jefferson National Forest, Blacksburg Ranger District.
Management status: 10,753-acre wilderness and 5,976 acres in three nonwilderness roadless additions.
Ecosystems: Eastern deciduous forest.
Elevation range: 2,100 to 4,128 feet.
System trails: 29.5 miles.
Maximum core-to-perimeter distance: 2 miles.
Activities: Hiking, backpacking, and hunting.
Modes of travel: Foot.
Maps: Blacksburg Ranger District map; Eggleston-VA, Interior-VA and WVA, Newport-VA and WVA, and Waiteville-VA and WVA 1:24,000 topo maps.

OVERVIEW: Mountain Lake is a wonderfully rugged area just a short drive north from Blacksburg in southwest Virginia. The wilderness crosses four major ridges: Little Mountain, Potts Mountain, Johns Creek Mountain, and Salt Pond Mountain. This is high-country Virginia; the crests of Potts and Salt Pond mountains rise above 4,000 feet. Just as the peaks are high, the hillsides are steep. The Appalachian Trail climbs 1,700 vertical feet in the short stretch from the War Spur Shelter to Lone Pine Peak. In years past the AT climbed this ridge in a hurry. Although still a tough climb, relocation of the trail has broken up the climb by way of several long grades. The sandstone backbones of several of these ridges offer good views, making the climbs worth it. Bear Cliff and War Spur Overlook are two examples. The high elevations and deep valleys conspire to create unique ecosystems in Mountain Lake. Oak-hickory forest dominates most of Mountain Lake Wilderness, but stands of tall cove hardwoods grow in protected pockets. Elsewhere, old pastures are slowly being reclaimed by succession. There is a small stand of virgin timber in the upper reaches of the War Spur Branch, which contains birch, hemlock, and red spruce. A field of ferns along the Appalachian Trail between Potts Mountain and Lone Pine Peak surrounds Manns Bog. The bog is an anomaly in Virginia and is one of Old Dominion's few examples of the mountain bog ecosystem.

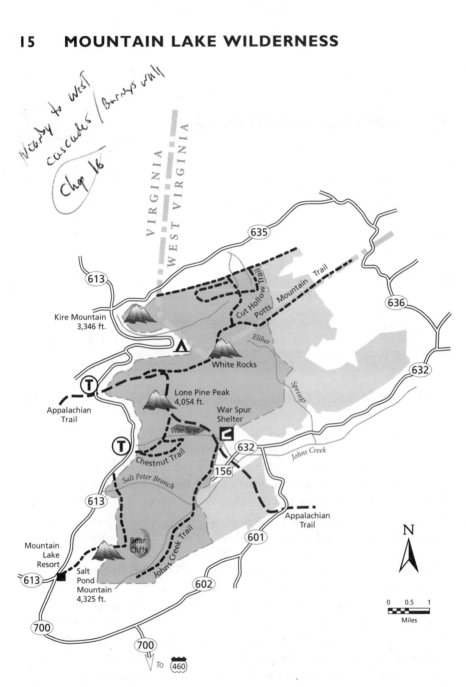

Nearby to west cascades/Barneys wall
Chap 16

VIRGINIA
WEST VIRGINIA

613

635

636

Kire Mountain
3,346 ft.

Cut Hollow Trail

Potts Mountain Trail

632

Eliber

White Rocks

Appalachian
Trail

Lone Pine Peak
4,054 ft.

Springs

War Spur
Shelter

War Spur

632

Johns Creek

Chestnut Trail

156

Salt Peter Branch

613

Appalachian
Trail

601

Mountain
Lake
Resort

Bear
Cliffs

Johns Creek Trail

613

Salt
Pond
Mountain
4,325 ft.

602

700

700

To 460

N

0   0.5   1
Miles

The rocky War Spur Overlook offers spectacular views into the War Spur and Johns Creek valleys.

Mountain Lake has excellent opportunities for camping and backpacking. Old pastures along Potts Mountain Trail make wonderful campsites, and water is reasonably available throughout the wilderness. White Rocks Campground is located on the northwestern edge of the wilderness just off County Road 613 and has facilities for car camping. For visitors looking for a romantic weekend, or maybe just a few more amenities than a backpack can hold, Mountain Lake Resort offers upscale accommodations in a beautiful setting. From the resort, trailheads are just a short drive away.

RECREATIONAL USES: The primary activities in Mountain Lake are hiking and hunting. The extensive trail system contains a variety of long and short hikes, providing excellent opportunities for both day hikers and backpackers. The Appalachian Trail sees a yearly migration of through-hikers during May and June; the War Spur Shelter located at the southeastern boundary of the wilderness is busy this time of year. Most major hunting seasons, including deer, bear, and turkey seasons, draw hunters in good numbers. Mountain Lake Wilderness is also used for scientific research. The University of Virginia's biological station along the border of the wilderness is used for summer-session classes as well as a headquarters for field research.

Day Hike

Chestnut Trail

Distance: 2.5 miles.
Difficulty: Easy.
Topo map: Interior-VA and WVA.

HOW TO GET THERE: From Interstate 81 near Christiansburg, take exit 118B and drive west on US 460 toward Blacksburg. Follow US 460 past Blacksburg 20.3 miles to County Road 700 on the right (north). A sign for Mountain Lake marks this intersection. Turn right and drive 6.9 miles north to Mountain Lake Resort, where CR 700 becomes CR 613. After passing the resort, Mountain Lake Wilderness is on the right side of the road. Continue 3.1 miles to the trailhead and parking lot for Chestnut Trail on the right.

The Chestnut Trail, although a short walk, provides access to a pair of Mountain Lake's unique sights: virgin timber and an expansive vista. The hike is easy and is appropriate for both adults and children.

A sign at the trailhead gives directions and mileages to nearby trails. Chestnut Trail begins just to the right of this sign. The trail enters an oak and poplar forest and travels downhill to a small bridge. Cross the bridge and push up a short hill to a signed junction with the War Spur Overlook Trail. Don't forgo the opportunity to soak in the view at War Spur Overlook. The detour is only 0.2 mile and is well worth the effort. The side trail drops away from the Chestnut Trail and soon ends at a rock outcrop with beautiful views of the War Spur Branch drainage and Johns Mountain to the east.

After sunning on the rocks for a while, remember there is still a virgin forest to see. Travel back up the War Spur Overlook Trail and continue out on the Chestnut Trail. The trail descends steeply into the untouched stand. A unique forest type in Virginia, the only thing that matches the age of the red spruce and yellow birch is their majesty.

After crossing a log bridge, the trail moves into a stand of mixed hardwoods. In another mile, the path intersects the War Spur Trail. A right here leads to the Appalachian Trail. Instead, turn left to head back to the trailhead.

Day Hike or Overnight Backpack

Appalachian Trail to War Spur Shelter

Distance: 7.8 miles round-trip.
Difficulty: Strenuous.
Topo maps: Interior-VA and WVA, and Waiteville-VA and WVA.

HOW TO GET THERE: From Interstate 81 near Christiansburg, take exit 118B and drive west on US 460 toward Blacksburg. Follow US 460 past Blacksburg 20.3 miles to County Road 700 on the right (north). A sign for Mountain Lake marks this intersection. Turn right and drive 6.9 miles north to Mountain Lake Resort, where CR 700 becomes CR 613. After passing the resort, Mountain Lake Wilderness is on the right side of the road. Continue 4 miles to the trailhead and parking lot for the AT on the left.

This section of the AT is a good example of why the trail is sometimes referred to as a "wilderness trail." The trail travels through the heart of Mountain Lake Wilderness; those strong enough to contend with Potts Mountain are rewarded with a sheltered campsite and high mountain vistas. This 3.9-mile section may seem short to some, but the rugged nature of the hike and the existence of a shelter and water source at the wilderness boundary make the War Spur a nice overnight destination. As with the entire 2,138-mile length of the AT, frequent white blazes mark the route. You can thank the Roanoke Appalachian Trail Club for the blazes in this section. The RATC maintains the AT and many side trails in Mountain Lake Wilderness.

From the parking lot, the trail enters the woods near a Forest Service information stand. The AT climbs an easy grade as it parallels the Potts Mountain Trail, passing Wind Rock and providing good views of Peters Mountain. The AT soon bends right and leaves Potts Mountain Trail behind. As the AT falls away from the crest of Potts Mountain and climbs easily back across 4,054-foot Lone Pine Peak, it passes through a lovely stand of hemlock and ferns.

After Lone Pine Peak, the AT begins the downhill drop to War Spur Shelter. In the past, this section of trail was steep. Your knees will thank the Appalachian Trail Conference for its decision to relocate the trail by including several switchbacks along this rugged hillside. The next landmark is the intersection with the 1.5-mile War Spur Connector Trail, where a sign marks distances. It is 2.6 miles back to CR 613; the War Spur Shelter is 1.3 miles ahead. The forest here contains oak and hickory, but as the trail descends, the ridge becomes drier and tree species change to chestnut oak and white pine. At the shelter, War Spur Branch offers filterable water to the trail weary. Down the ridge another 0.9 mile is Forest Road 156. For the remainder of the day, you can sit back, read a book, listen to the stream babble and the wind whisper, and rejuvenate your soul.

Note: The proximity of Peters Mountain Wilderness (see chapter 17) to Mountain Lake provides the opportunity for backpackers to explore both areas from the AT. The AT travels about 29 miles from CR 641 near Narrows, Virginia, to FR 156. There are three shelters in this section. From FR 156, distances are as follows: War Spur Shelter, 0.9 mile; Bailey Gap Shelter, 8.7 miles;

and Pine Swamp Shelter, 12.7 miles. The longest section is the portion be-tween the Pine Swamp Branch Shelter and CR 641, which clocks in at 16.6 miles. With cars parked at opposite ends, you could create a rewarding hike of two to four days. The shelters help to keep pack weight down by allowing you to leave the tent at home. Be aware, however, that from late April to early June, a string of through-hikers moves north along the AT, and shelters could be crowded.

Cascades Roadless Area

Location: 40 miles west of Roanoke, Virginia; about 5 miles northeast of the town of Pembroke.
Size: 1,833 acres.
Administration: USDAFS Jefferson National Forest, Blacksburg Ranger District.
Management status: Nonwilderness roadless area and national recreation trail.
Ecosystems: Eastern deciduous forest.
Elevation range: 2,300 to 4,000 feet.
System trails: 5.6 miles.
Maximum core-to-perimeter distance: 1.5 miles.
Activities: Hiking and photography.
Modes of travel: Foot.
Maps: Blacksburg Ranger District map; Eggleston-VA 1:24,000 topo map.

OVERVIEW: Although small, the Cascades Roadless Area is one of the most scenic wildlands in the state. Much of the area's natural beauty was created by Little Stony Creek as it carved through the neighboring mountains. This fast-flowing creek tumbles from its headwaters on Lone Pine Peak to the New River at Pembroke. On its way, the creek plummets over the Cascades, a 66-foot waterfall that plunges into a sparkling pool.

Below the falls, Little Stony Creek cuts through a narrow gorge with towering cliffs and steep canyon walls. During extremely cold winters, the falls and the creek freeze over, forming spectacular ice columns. The Forest Service has determined that a 3.2-mile segment of Little Stony Creek within the roadless area is eligible for designation under the Wild and Scenic Rivers Act.

Towering cliffs are another trademark of this roadless area. The most notable is Barneys Wall. These massive cliffs form a barrier along the northwestern edge of the roadless area running along the southeastern ridge of Butt Mountain. Barneys Wall provides a commanding view of the New River Valley.

The area is also rich in Appalachian vegetation. Along with a profusion of wildflowers in the spring and summer, walking fern and Jeffersonian twin-leaf grow here. The region also supports about 660 acres of potential old-growth forest. Tall cove hardwoods line Little Stony Creek. Sugar maple and red maple are found in abundance, and several varieties of oak and hickory are represented in the overstory. Dogwood and serviceberry thrive in the understory, and thickets of rhododendron climb the steep canyon walls.

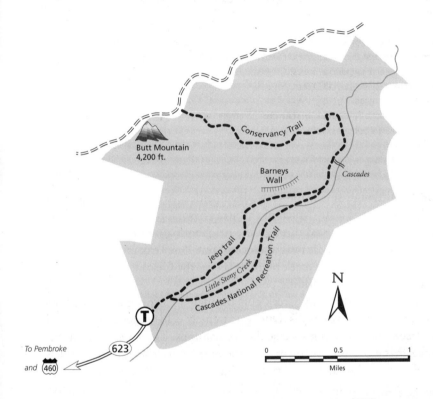

Butt Mountain
4,200 ft.

Conservancy Trail

Barneys
Wall

Cascades

Jeep trail

Little Stony Creek

Cascades National Recreation Trail

T

To Pembroke
and 460

623

N

0   0.5   1
Miles

The Cascades Trail rewards hikers with beautiful views of the Cascades of Little Stony Creek.

RECREATIONAL USES: The major recreational activity in this roadless area is hiking. Cascades National Recreation Trail, which parallels Little Stony Creek from the trailhead to the Cascades, is a favorite destination for hikers throughout the state. The waterfall provides ample opportunity to experience one of the finest natural wonders in western Virginia. Anglers enjoy fishing for trout in the creek's many pools and rapids, and photographers find plenty of scenery within the confines of Little Stony Creek's narrow gorge. Add the 3.7-mile Conservancy Trail to your itinerary to reach the ridge crest of Butt Mountain and Barneys Wall, another good site for spectacular photography.

The only drawback to the Cascades Roadless Area is its popularity. The Cascades Trail is frequently crowded, as is the area around the falls. If solitude is what you seek, rarely is it found in this area.

Day Hike

Cascades National Recreation Trail

Distance: 3.8 miles round-trip.
Difficulty: Easy.
Topo map: Eggleston-VA.

HOW TO GET THERE: From Blacksburg, drive 19 miles west on US 460 to Pembroke. At the Cascades National Recreation Trail sign, turn right on County Road 623. Drive 3.6 miles north to the trailhead and parking lot at the Cascades Picnic Area.

Cascades National Recreation Trail begins at the Cascades Picnic Area. There is a Forest Service information center near the trailhead. The trail enters the woods and begins to parallel Little Stony Creek. The creek is strewn with boulders, and the water tumbles over the stones in a multitude of small falls. Anglers can pit their skills against the native trout that thrive in these waters. At 0.4 mile an old jeep trail continues straight; turn right and cross the creek on a small footbridge. The trail then turns left and continues upstream on the south bank of the creek. About 1.2 miles from the first footbridge, another footbridge crosses the creek.

Continue upstream about 0.3 mile to reach the Cascades. The waterfall is nestled in a bowl at the mouth of a narrow gorge. The water is cool and refreshing after the hike. *One note of caution:* Climbing behind the falls is prohibited and extremely dangerous. The rocks are wet and slippery, and falling from this spot can result in death.

To return to the trailhead, either walk back along the Cascades Trail or climb the slope at the entrance to the bowl to an old jeep trail. Follow this old road south to rejoin the trail at the first footbridge, 0.4 mile from the trailhead.

Peters Mountain Wilderness

Location: 9 miles northwest of Blacksburg, Virginia.
Size: 7,732 acres.
Administration: USDAFS Jefferson National Forest, Blacksburg Ranger District.
Management status: 3,326-acre wilderness and 4,406-acre nonwilderness roadless land.
Ecosystems: Oak-hickory forest.
Elevation range: 2,098 feet to 3,956 feet.
System trails: 20.2 miles.
Maximum core-to-perimeter distance: 1.6 miles.
Activities: Hiking and backpacking.
Modes of travel: Foot.
Maps: Blacksburg District map; Interior-VA and WVA, and Lindside-VA and WVA 1:24,000 topo maps.

OVERVIEW: Although Peters Mountain Wilderness is one of Virginia's smaller wilderness areas, neighboring nonwilderness roadless areas help to increase the acreage and the available hiking miles. The wilderness area hangs on a slice of eastern slope on Peters Mountain. The area is bordered to the northeast and southwest by two wilderness additions. The northeastern Wilderness Addition B is the larger of the two, at 2,906 acres. These dry statistics mean one thing: more wild Virginia to enjoy.

Simple geography makes Peters Mountain wonderfully rugged. Trails in the area are of two types: those that run *along* the top of the mountain, and those that run *to* the top of the mountain. If you're hiking the latter, chances are you're breathing hard and hoping to get to the former pretty soon. The trails that travel up the ridge follow stream drainages and gain altitude rapidly. Groundhog Trail, for example, averages an 8 to 12 percent grade—a tough, sustained climb for any hiker. Topography played savior to trees, though, as there are stands of virgin timber on the steeper slopes and in deeper hollows. An experienced off-trail hiker can find these quiet forests tucked away from the daypacks and backpacks of trail hikers.

Although several intermittent streams trickle through this wilderness, there are two main drainages, Dismal Branch and Pine Swamp Branch, both of which empty into Stony Creek. Water is abundant at lower elevations, but is extremely scarce at the ridge top.

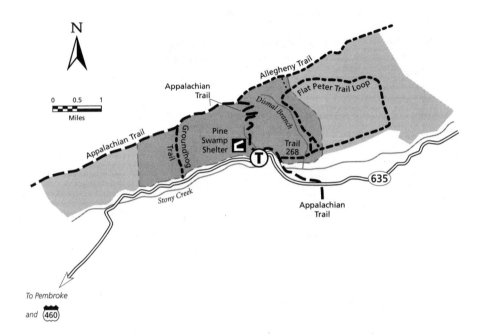

Perhaps in part owing to its ruggedness, Peters Mountain is a beautiful area to visit. The southern crest is strewn with sandstone outcrops, and there are views west into West Virginia. Winter offers crisp, clean air and the best opportunities for solitude. For one of Virginia's smaller wilderness areas, it's easy to "lose" yourself on this pristine mountain.

RECREATIONAL USES: Backpacking and hiking are the major pastimes in this wilderness area. In late April a string of through-hikers makes its way across the mountain along the Appalachian Trail en route to Maine. Hikers along the AT should note that older maps show the trail taking a direct route up the ridge along Pine Swamp Branch. The trail has been moved in this area and now makes several long switchbacks along the flank of Pine Swamp Ridge. The wilderness also sees hiking use by college students from nearby Blacksburg. Flat Peter Trail Loop in the northern wilderness addition is a particularly scenic hike and draws the majority of day hikers to the area. Visitors to the wilderness in fall and early winter should be cautious, as hunting seasons bring many hunters. Stony Creek, running along the base of Peters Mountain, is a popular trout stream among local anglers.

Day Hike

Appalachian Trail/Flat Peter Trail Loop

Distance: 8.4 miles.
Difficulty: Strenuous.
Topo map: Interior-VA and WVA.

HOW TO GET THERE: From Interstate 81 at Christiansburg, take exit 118B to US 460 west toward Blacksburg. Travel 30.2 miles and turn right onto County Road 635. Drive 9.8 miles and park on the left side of the road at the Appalachian Trailhead.

This loop combines three trails—the Appalachian, Allegheny, and Flat Peter—and a short bushwhack to tour around Pine Swamp Ridge in the northern half of the wilderness. The hike begins and ends at the lower trailhead for the Appalachian Trail. A bridge crosses Stony Creek just past the parking lot.

From the parking lot, the AT moves into the woods near an information stand. In the past, the given distance to the intersection with the Allegheny Trail was 1.3 miles. This was true when the AT followed Pine Swamp Branch all the way to the crest of the ridge. Now that the AT makes a series of switchbacks up Pine Swamp Ridge, the distance is closer to 2.5 miles.

Pine Swamp Branch Shelter.

Follow the spur trail from the parking lot to the AT and bear left. The trail travels up the ridge about 0.3 mile to the Pine Swamp Branch Shelter. Then the trail becomes rocky as it follows Pine Swamp Branch. About 1 mile from the shelter the trail forks and the old AT route separates off to the left. Take the right-hand fork and follow the "new" AT route as it crosses the creek and then starts up the ridge. To climb Pine Swamp Ridge, the AT twists through a series of about fifteen switchbacks, each leg a little longer than the previous one. Finally, the AT levels out and reaches the saddle between Pine Swamp Ridge and Peters Mountain. Here the AT intersects the Allegheny Trail.

Turn right at this junction. The Allegheny Trail, marked with yellow blazes, travels northeast along the ridge top. After 0.8 mile, the trail widens to a jeep road. Continue to follow this "trail" another 0.7 mile. About 1.3 miles from the AT, the Allegheny Trail leaves the wilderness. A sign marks the boundary.

From this point the hike runs downhill. This first section, however, is a 0.4-mile bushwhack. The best route to follow is across the saddle between Huckleberry Ridge and Peters Mountain. Although turning right and just hiking downhill will get you to the Flat Peter Trail, the slope of the saddle is friendlier. At the wilderness boundary sign, turn right and follow the finger ridge across the saddle. The intersection with the Flat Peter Trail lies about midway between the two peaks.

When the Flat Peter Trail is reached, turn right (southwest). This trail is also marked with yellow blazes. The trail drops down to Dismal Branch then follows it down the mountain. On its way, there will be about ten creek crossings. This section of trail travels through rhododendron tunnels and hardwood forests with lush green understory. As the trail nears the base of the ridge, look for a clearing to the left if you're interested in an excellent campsite. Past this clearing, be on the lookout for the intersection with Trail 268, which branches right and returns to the AT. Follow Trail 268's easy grade to the AT, turn right, and walk the AT. There is a section of short, steep hills, the last of which brings the hiker back down to Stony Creek. After a flat stretch, a rhododendron tunnel leads to the AT where it joins the parking lot access trail. Turn left here to return to the parking area.

Backpack

Appalachian Trail

Distance: 16.4 miles round-trip.
Difficulty: Strenuous.
Topo maps: Interior-VA and WVA, and Lindside-VA and WVA.

HOW TO GET THERE: From Interstate 81 at Christiansburg, take exit 118B to US 460 west toward Blacksburg. Travel 30.2 miles and turn right onto County Road 635. Drive 11.5 miles and park on the left side of the road at the Cherokee Flats Appalachian Trailhead. (Parking at the lower trailhead described earlier cuts about 2.5 miles one way off the hike.)

Peters Mountain is blessed with the AT running through the heart of the area. This section of the AT is extremely well maintained by volunteers from the Virginia Tech Outing Club. The AT travels the spine of Peters Mountain proper, and then descends the ridge to CR 635. Pine Swamp Branch Shelter is located near CR 635 and is a great overnight destination. Hiking along this trail is not easy, however. The crest is rocky and the ridge presents a long series of switchbacks. The rewards are abundant, though, and include views into West Virginia and a walk along a babbling mountain stream.

From the Cherokee Flats parking area, the AT enters a forest of hemlock and rhododendron. The trail is easy to follow and is marked by the well-known white blazes. The first section runs along Stony Creek southwest to the Pine Swamp Branch Shelter. There are a few intersections with side trails, but stay on the AT by following the white blazes.

Shortly after the Pine Swamp Branch Shelter, the AT splits with the old route of the AT. The new route crosses Pine Swamp Branch and then climbs

Pine Swamp Ridge through a series of about fifteen switchbacks. This ups the mileage from the lower parking lot to the crest to 2.5 miles, a substantial increase from the old 1.3-mile route. At the crest, the AT intersects the Allegheny Trail. There is a sign at this intersection giving distances to Groundhog Trail (3.9 miles) and US 460 (16.9 miles). Follow the white-blazed AT as it branches left and to the southwest.

From this point the AT travels the ridge top. There are short ups and downs, and harsh winters produce a substantial amount of downed timber. Water is hard to come by up here, so be sure to pack some in. The trail passes several large boulders, and there are some views into West Virginia. The trail drops down into Dickenson Gap and, after 5.4 miles, reaches Groundhog Trail. A left onto Groundhog Trail leads down the ridge to CR 635, but that leaves a long hike on the road back to the parking lot and trailhead.

Instead, stay on the AT as it climbs steeply back to the ridge top. From here it continues out the crest along a series of rock outcrops and then reaches the wilderness boundary. Camp here and then backtrack the way you came, or drop down Groundhog Trail and hike the road (or jockey a prearranged vehicle shuttle). You could also forge onward to US 460 some 10 miles ahead. In any event, you can't lose—you're enjoying a nice hike, after all.

Note: With the availability of the trail shelters and the nearby Mountain Lake Wilderness, an extended backpack through both wilderness regions is possible. There are four trail shelters along a 30-mile section of the AT between US 460 near Narrows and Forest Road 156 just past Mountain Lake Wilderness. For mileage information and shelter names, see the Appalachian Trail description in Mountain Lake Wilderness, chapter 15.

Kimberling Creek Wilderness ██ 18

Location: 17 miles north of Wytheville, Virginia; about 10 miles northeast of the town of Bland.
Size: 5,580 acres.
Administration: USDAFS Jefferson National Forest, Wythe Ranger District.
Management status: Wilderness area.
Ecosystems: Eastern deciduous forest.
Elevation range: 2,250 to 3,200 feet.
System trails: Approximately 4 miles of unmaintained trails.
Maximum core-to-perimeter distance: 2.5 miles.
Activities: Hiking, bushwhacking, hunting, and fishing.
Modes of travel: Foot.
Maps: Wythe Ranger District Sportsman's map; Rocky Gap-VA 1:24,000 topo map.

OVERVIEW: Kimberling Creek Wilderness is a 5,580-acre area located in the Wythe Ranger District of the Jefferson National Forest. Nearby Kimberling Creek, which flows outside the wilderness boundary, nevertheless gives the area its name. Congress declared Kimberling Creek a wilderness in 1984.

Kimberling Creek Wilderness hugs the southern flank and shoulder of Hogback Mountain up to the ridge top, which forms the northern border. Sulphur Spring Fork and Forest Road 281 form the southern boundary of the wilderness. North Fork, a small creek flowing from a spring high on Hogback Mountain, is the main drainage running through the heart of the wilderness. It feeds directly into Kimberling Creek. Other smaller spring-fed creeks drain into Sulphur Spring Fork at the southeastern end of the wilderness.

Most of Kimberling Creek Wilderness is forested in oak and hickory. Creek coves shelter towering poplar, white pine, and hemlock. Rhododendron and dogwood are also found in great abundance. You may even see an occasional pawpaw, a relict tree from the days when Virginia had a more tropical climate.

Kimberling Creek Wilderness is a remote, rugged, undeveloped area. The North Fork region has sustained a tremendous amount of storm damage, and hiking here is difficult at best. Travel at your own risk. An injury in the backcountry could prove fatal, and help is far away. It's best to hike with a friend if you plan to travel through this area.

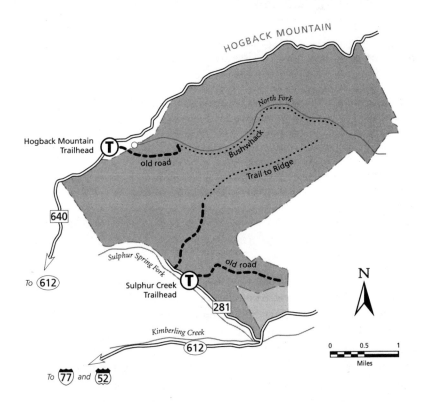

RECREATIONAL USES: Recreation in Kimberling Creek Wilderness is limited due to the lack of maintained trails. It is possible to hike throughout this region and not see another human being. The wilderness is completely undeveloped; the trails described here are the remains of old abandoned roads and an old railroad grade. Many of the hikes are difficult because of the primitive nature of the area.

For the more adventurous, however, this remoteness is also Kimberling Creek's major advantage. About 3 miles of old roads wander within the wilderness boundary. An old railroad grade follows the North Fork for about 3 miles. All other hiking opportunities are cross-country journeys that should only be done with a good map and compass and the skill to use them well.

Day Hike

Sulphur Spring Trail
Distance: 3.2 miles round-trip.
Difficulty: Easy.
Topo map: Rocky Gap-VA.

HOW TO GET THERE: From the junction of Interstates 81 and 77 near Wytheville, drive north about 6 miles on I–77 to exit 48 and turn right at the stop sign. Drive 0.8 mile, turn left onto US 52, and drive 3.9 miles north. Turn right on County Road 612, drive 3.9 miles east, and turn left (north) on Forest Road 281. Go 1 mile to a parking lot on the left by a gate. Please park off to the side and do not block the gate.

This trail is a short out-and-back that follows an old road into the lower southern corner of the wilderness. To reach the trailhead, hike north up FR 281 about 50 yards, crossing the creek, and look for the trail on the right. The trail follows a gentle contour along Sulphur Spring Fork. You might notice some storm damage along the trail, but it is not impossible to get around. After about 0.5 mile, the trail climbs over a low ridge and enters another little creek drainage. Tall white pine, hemlock, and poplar dominate the area. The trail bends to the right and enters a dry streambed just before reaching the wilderness boundary. If you are so inclined, there are many nice sites along the trail in which to camp.

Day Hike

Trail to the Ridge

Distance: 2 miles round-trip, more if exploring the ridge top.
Difficulty: Easy.
Topo map: Rocky Gap-VA.

HOW TO GET THERE: Follow the directions for the Sulphur Spring trail above. From the gate, walk about 0.4 mile north up Forest Road 281 to a small meadow on the right. The trail begins at the base of the hill.

This trail shows only light use and at times is indistinct and hard to follow. It does, however, provide quick access to the ridge top, where there are many good bushwhacking opportunities. A good map and compass are required for any backcountry travel here.

After crossing the field, the trail begins a steep and steady climb with just one brief flat section about midway. As the trail nears the ridge, the forest changes from cove hardwoods and hemlock to the drier species such as chestnut oak, pitch pine, and hickory. Near the top, the oaks and hickories become much larger. Once on the ridge top, you can enjoy a pleasant walk along the ridge to the northeast. The crest is open and easily traveled, with panoramic views to the east. The ridge makes a series of short ups and downs, with a gradual overall decline in elevation. Just before dropping to the North Fork, the ridge narrows markedly. There is a beautiful spot to camp near the end of the ridge, but there is no water here. The distance from the trailhead to the end of the ridge is about 3.2 miles.

Day Hike

Ridge Top to North Fork Trail (Bushwhack)

Distance: 2.4 miles round-trip, more if exploring the North Fork area.
Difficulty: Moderate to strenuous, depending on destination.
Topo map: Rocky Gap-VA.

HOW TO GET THERE: From the junction of Interstates 81 and 77 near Wytheville, drive north about 6 miles on I–77 to exit 48 and turn right at the stop sign. Drive 0.8 mile, turn left onto US 52, and drive 3.9 miles north. Turn right on County Road 612 and drive 0.3 mile east to Forest Road 640, which is rough and not recommended for low-clearance vehicles. Turn left onto FR 640 and drive 4.6 miles north and east to a small parking lot on the right.

Looking east from a ridge in Kimberling Creek Wilderness.

The trail begins at the top of Hogback Mountain, where the forest species include chestnut oak, hickory, maple, and white pine, and descends to the North Fork. A short distance from the road there is an earthen barrier; just beyond it is a small road to the right, which dies out after about 0.2 mile. Continue straight at this junction. The road drops gradually for about 1.5 miles, then drops more abruptly to the North Fork.

After a switchback to the left, the dry forest gives way to cove hardwoods, hemlock, and white pine, as well as many large rhododendrons. Once at the creek, a left turn leads upstream to the spring for the North Fork; a right leads downstream. Either direction is a major bushwhack.

The hike downstream is rugged. This is probably one of the most remote areas found in the Virginia wilderness system. Major storm damage along parts of the creek slow your progress. It is necessary at times to either crawl under or climb over all the downfall.

Towering cliffs line the stream, which is littered with large, flat stones. There is also an old railroad grade along the creek, as evidenced by sections of railroad ties, steel rails, and washed-out bridge abutments. When you've had enough scrambling, retrace your bushwhack to the old road and climb back up to the top of Hogback Mountain.

Brushy Mountain Roadless Area   19

Location: 4 miles north of Bland, Virginia.
Size: 4,183 acres.
Administration: USDAFS Jefferson National Forest, Wythe Ranger District.
Management status: Nonwilderness roadless area.
Ecosystems: Eastern deciduous forest.
Elevation range: 2,280 to 3,250 feet.
System trails: 6.9 miles.
Maximum core-to-perimeter distance: 2.4 miles.
Activities: Hiking, bushwhacking, camping, orienteering, hunting, and fishing.
Modes of travel: Foot.
Maps: Wythe Ranger District sportsman's map; Bland-VA and Rocky Gap-VA 1:24,000 topo maps.

OVERVIEW: The Brushy Mountain Roadless area is a 4,183-acre region in the Wythe Ranger District of the Jefferson National Forest. The roadless area is located just south of Kimberling Creek Wilderness and just North of Bland, Virginia, in the eastern portion of Bland County.

The Brushy Mountain Roadless Area encompasses the southern end of Brushy Mountain and a long narrow panhandle that stretches to the north. Lying in the Ridge and Valley Province of Virginia, the area is characterized by steep side slopes and narrow ridge crests. These steep slopes create the many small feeder creeks for Kimberling Creek on the western boundary and Helvey's Mill Creek to the east.

The vegetation of Brushy Mountain is mainly a broadleaf deciduous forest with a scattering of white and yellow pine. The sheltered hollows provide refuge for tall stands of cove hardwoods.

RECREATIONAL USES: Hiking and hunting are the two major activities in the Brushy Mountain roadless area. Most of the hiking within the roadless area takes place on the Appalachian Trail. More than 6 miles of the AT pass through the area, and a short spur trail heads to Helvey's Shelter. This trail is well maintained and usually free of windfall. Most of the rest of the region is inaccessible because of steep slopes, but hunters can find access into the outer areas of this wild area by means of several roads along the boundaries.

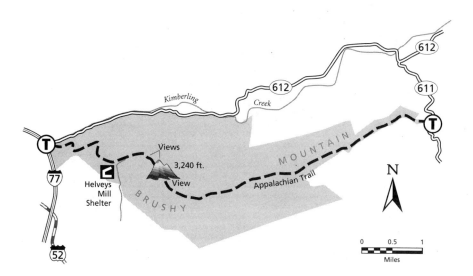

A rhododendron jungle.

Overnighter

Appalachian Trail

Distance: 5.6 miles round-trip.
Difficulty: Moderate.
Topo map: Rocky Gap-VA.

HOW TO GET THERE: Take Interstate 81 to 77 north to the Bland exit (exit 52) and turn right at the stop sign. Follow US 52/42 0.8 mile to a T intersection. Turn left on US 52 and continue 3.9 miles to a sharp left bend at the top of the mountain. Go straight on CR 612 and proceed 0.7 mile to a parking area on the right.

From the parking area, follow the white blazed AT into the woods, reaching a left bend after about 100 feet. The trail travels close to Kimberling Creek a short distance before crossing it, then begins a short climb up the right ridge slope. Rhododendron crowds the trail under a canopy of tall cove hardwoods and hemlock. Just after the creek crossing, a sign gives the distance to State Road 611: 7.75 miles. After the short climb, the path follows an old grade for a short distance, and the walking is easy.

At the end of this short flat section, the trail climbs at a moderate grade. After a right bend, enter a narrow hollow, continuing the climb. Several large oak trees thrive in this small hollow. After wrapping left around the end of the hollow, the climb becomes more difficult, but the end of the climb is near.

At the crest, the grade becomes easy. The trail turns abruptly to the right and crosses a narrow saddle. At the end of this saddle, a trail exits right, leading to a small private hunting camp. Remain on the AT as it meanders just to the east of the ridge crest and follows an old road grade.

At 1.7 miles a sign marks the blue blazed trail to the Helveys Mill Shelter. The shelter trail is an easy 0.25 mile. The shelter has a privy and picnic table, and water can be found down the hill just past the shelter. There are also several campsites in this area.

The AT continues on the old road past the shelter trail. This section is an easy stroll on a tree-lined trail. About 0.4 mile past the shelter trail, there are two views to the north of the Kimberling Creek Wilderness. Past these view sheds, there is a slight climb. The trail exits the road to the left and begins a short steep climb to the summit of Brushy Mountain. Approximately 2.8 miles from the trailhead, the summit provides a wonderful view of the Kimberling Creek Valley and the panhandle of Brushy Mountain. The mountain to the east of the panhandle is Big Walker Mountain. From here it is possible to continue on the AT 4.7 miles to CR 611 or turn around and head back to the parking area.

Little Walker Mountain Roadless Area 20

Location: 7 miles west of Pulaski, Virginia.
Size: 9,815 acres.
Administration: USDAFS Jefferson National Forest, Wythe Ranger District.
Management status: Nonwilderness roadless area.
Ecosystems: Eastern deciduous forest.
Elevation range: 2,080 to 3,120 feet.
System trails: 5.5 miles of maintained trail and several miles of old road that are suitable for hiking.
Maximum core-to-perimeter distance: 3.2 miles.
Activities: Hiking, hunting, fishing, horseback riding, and mountain biking.
Modes of travel: Foot, mountain bike, and horse.
Maps: Wythe Ranger District sportsman's map; Long Spur-VA and Pulaski-VA 1:24,000 topo maps.

OVERVIEW: The Little Walker Mountain area is bounded on the northwest by the long, low-running ridge of Little Walker Mountain; Tract Mountain forms the southern edge of the roadless area. In the sheltered valley between the two ridges lies the Tract Fork. This narrow, clear flowing brook is a Class III native trout stream. The entire area encompasses more than 9,800 acres.

The roadless area contains one of the last few remaining pure stands of table mountain pine in Virginia. Oak and hickory tend to dominate the ridges; yellow pine is well established on the drier sites. The sheltered coves contain large stands of cove hardwoods and tall white pine. The endangered swordleaf phlox grows within the boundaries of the roadless area.

Dry, steep slopes characterize the western side of Little Walker Mountain. The crest of this long ridge is dominated by chestnut oak and small pine. Mountain laurel and blueberry thickets thrive near the summit of the crest. The ridge itself rises and falls, with a gradual decrease in elevation along the northern end of the ridge.

Tract Mountain lies along the southern end of the proposed wilderness. Tall, knurled hardwoods dominate the crest of this ridge. In places the area has almost a parklike feeling. There are several small unnamed trails (approximately 7 miles) along the crest of Tract Mountain that provide easy access to this beautiful, pristine area.

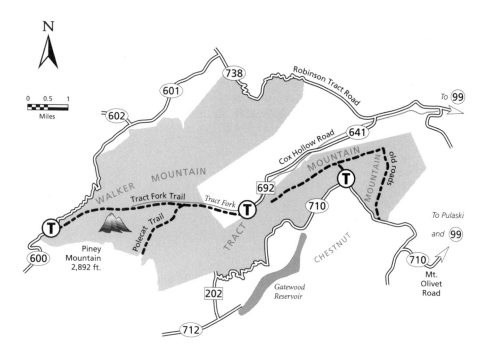

The Tract Fork is heavily shaded by rhododendron, with large hemlocks, white pine, and cove hardwoods towering above. The Tract Fork is completely unspoiled from its forested headwaters down to the uppermost ford, a distance of about 2.25 miles. Near the headwaters of Tract Fork is the 2,892-foot summit of the appropriately named Piney Mountain, which is dominated by a thick stand of small pine. Peak Creek finds its beginnings on the southern slope of Little Walker Mountain. The Tract Fork and Peak Creek both support wild trout populations.

RECREATIONAL USES: Little Walker Mountain supports a wide variety of recreational activities. Hunters can find ample game; the region supports a large wild turkey population, while white-tailed deer thrive throughout the region. The trail network offers challenging day hikes and quiet solitude along the old road on Tract Mountain. Mountain biking and horseback riding are also popular activities in the Little Walker Mountain area.

Day Hike

Tract Fork Trail

Distance: 8 miles round-trip.
Difficulty: Moderate.
Topo maps: Long Spur-VA and Pulaski-VA.

HOW TO GET THERE: Take Interstate 81 to exit 94 and turn right at the stop sign. Travel west on Virginia Highway 99 which becomes County Road 738 (Robinson Tract Road) at the Pulaski city limits. After approximately 4 miles, turn left on CR 641 (Cox Hollow Road). Watch carefully for Cox Hollow Road, as it is easy to miss. Proceed 4 miles to the end of the road. There are two shallow fords to cross near the end of the road.

The Tract Fork Trail begins at the end of the parking lot. The trail on the left is a dead end. Initially, the Tract Fork Trail is weedy, but the way is clear. Within 100 yards, you'll leave the weeds behind and enter the woods. The trail, marked with yellow diamonds, follows an old road. The clear flowing Tract Fork is on the left, and many small, still pools of water lie under a canopy of rhododendron. Straight white pine and cove hardwoods in turn shelter the rhododendron.

About 0.75 mile from the trailhead, the trail reaches the first of four quick creek crossings, none of which is difficult. After the third crossing, the Polecat Trail exits to the left. This 1.5-mile trail climbs quickly to the crest of Tract Mountain, descends sharply into a narrow steep-walled hollow, then follows an old grade that descends gradually to CR 707.

After the last creek crossing, the Tract Fork Trail continues to climb up the heart of the valley, but the complexion of the trail changes. Short drops to dry feeder streams followed by long moderate climbs characterize this next section of trail. Cross several of these feeders before coming to a small clearing in the early stages of forest succession. Small scrub pines are slowly changing the nature of the clearing, which is about 2.25 miles from the trailhead. A short side trail leads to the summit of Piney Mountain.

Beyond the clearing, under towering white pine, the Tract Fork Trail begins a moderate climb up the eastern slope of Little Walker Mountain. Near the crest, the white pine gives way to smaller oaks and yellow pine. The trail reaches the crest (3,120 feet) at about 3.25 miles. There are some limited views to the east and west from the crest.

The grade is now easy as the trail continues to follow the old road. Watch for an old forest road that turns back sharply to the left. Continue straight at this junction, after which the trail continues an easy descent to CR 600.

Day Hike

Old Mountain Roads Loop
Distance: 4.7 miles.
Difficulty: Moderate.
Topo map: Pulaski-VA.

HOW TO GET THERE: Take Interstate 81 to exit 94 and turn right at the stop sign. Take Virginia Highway 99 into Pulaski, following the Gatewood Reservoir signs. Turn left on Mt. Olivet Road and proceed 2.2 miles on CR 710; turn right at the Gatewood Reservoir sign. Continue 2.4 miles to a small parking area on the right.

This trail follows a series of old roads along Tract Mountain. The hike begins with a moderate climb to the crest of Tract Mountain at approximately 0.75 miles. Just before reaching the crest, the trail bends left.

On the crest it is possible to follow old roads right or left. The left road wanders along the crest of Tract Mountain to a dead end. There are a few small campsites along the trail. The crest provides a refuge for large, mature red oaks. There are limited summer views across the Tract Fork Valley to Little Walker Mountain to the west, and Brushy Ridge and Chestnut Mountain to the east.

Take the right fork, which meanders along the crest of Tract Mountain. In the early summer many wild turkeys nest along this road; watch carefully for the small chicks. The road turns right and begins a short moderate climb to the junction of another old forest road at 1.7 miles. At the junction, bear right and climb to the summit of Chestnut Mountain (elevation 2,814 feet). The crest of this ridge has sustained a great deal of storm damage; many large trees have been blown down or have lost large limbs.

Past the crest of Chestnut Mountain, the road begins a long steep descent to the road. At the road, turn right and walk 1.1 miles back to the parking area.

Beartown Wilderness

Location: 15 miles north of Marion, Virginia.
Size: 10,957 acres.
Administration: USDAFS Jefferson National Forest, Wythe Ranger District.
Management status: 6,375-acre wilderness and 4,582 nonwilderness roadless area.
Ecosystems: Eastern deciduous forest, with spruce and birch at higher elevations.
Elevation range: 2,200 to 4,710 feet.
System trails: 22 miles.
Maximum core-to-perimeter distance: 2.5 miles.
Activities: Hiking, camping, hunting, fishing, and photography.
Modes of travel: Foot.
Maps: Wythe Ranger District sportsman map; Hutchinson Rock-VA 1:24,000 topo map.

OVERVIEW: In contrast to the north-south trend of the Allegheny Mountains in northern Virginia, the southern end of the range slants nearly east to west. One mountain encompasses all of these directions as it curves completely around a 4- by 7-mile bowl known as Burkes Garden. This natural bowl is wrapped in the arms of Garden Mountain, about 15 miles north of Marion, Virginia. The Beartown Wilderness lies on the southwestern rim of Burkes Garden, bounded on the northwest by Clinch Mountain and on the southeast by Chestnut Ridge and Forest Road 222.

Garden Mountain is steep and rugged, with slopes approaching 80 degrees in some places. At 4,710 feet, it is also one of the highest summits in Virginia. The northern finger of Garden Mountain leads to Hutchinson Rock, a large cliff overlooking Burkes Garden to the east and Rich Mountain to the west.

Roaring Fork is the major drainage of the Beartown Wilderness. Coon Branch, Bearcamp Creek, and Cove Branch all feed into the Roaring Fork. Cove Branch has an unusual headwaters: a sphagnum bog nestled between Garden Mountain and Clinch Mountain at about 4,500 feet. The bog is almost completely surrounded by huge rhododendron thickets and low, impenetrable stands of hardwood. Protected by its remoteness, the bog is a beautiful reminder of how elevation, terrain, and moisture can combine to create a unique habitat. From here, Cove Branch tumbles over a series of rock ledges and small falls as it drops almost 1,300 feet in 2.5 miles. Cove hardwoods, such as yellow poplar and white oak, and tall hemlock and white pine are common

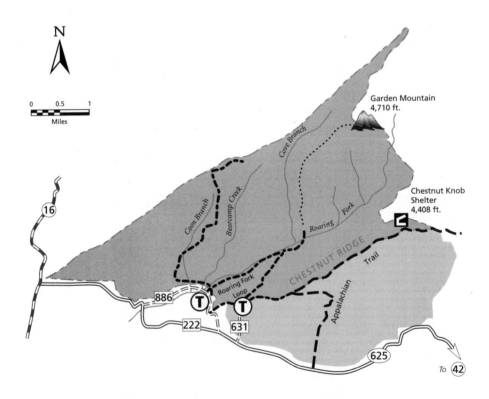

in sheltered creek bottoms. Oak-hickory forest blankets the eastern slope of Clinch Mountain, while chestnut oak dominates its ridge. Springs and creeks are numerous in this wilderness; water is readily available, but always treat it before drinking.

RECREATIONAL USES: The Beartown Wilderness is in a remote corner of the state with few modern access roads. Recreational use is limited to hiking, hunting, and fishing. The Appalachian Trail is the only maintained trail within the wilderness boundaries. Other trails follow old roads into the interior. These roads are being allowed to return to their natural condition, so expect downed timber and brush across the trails. This might slow your pace; allow extra time when hiking these routes.

The Roaring Fork supports a thriving community of fish, and anglers ply their skills in the cool waters of this pleasant creek. Hunters also enjoy the region, as there is a healthy deer and bear population. It is best to avoid this area during the general firearm season.

Day Hike

Roaring Fork Loop

Distance: 4 miles.
Difficulty: Moderate.
Topo map: Hutchinson Rock-VA.

HOW TO GET THERE: From the intersection of Interstates 77 and 81 near Wytheville, drive about 10 miles north on I–77 to exit 52. At the stop sign turn left (west) on US 52/Virginia Highway 42. Drive 4.2 miles west and turn right on VA 42. Continue 10.2 miles and turn right on County Road 625. This road forks in 0.4 mile; take the right-hand fork. Drive 7.6 miles north and west until you come to Forest Road 631 (CR 625 turns into Forest Road 222 during this stretch). Continue straight on FR 222 another 1.9 miles to a small road on the right. Watch carefully for this road, as it is unmarked and easy to miss. If you do not have a high-clearance vehicle, park and begin the hike here. Those traveling in a high-clearance vehicle can continue 1.3 miles north on this rugged road to the ford at Roaring Fork. A rock barrier marks the end of the road and the beginning of foot travel.

This trail is actually an old road that parallels the native trout waters of Roaring Fork. From the rock barrier, the trail crosses a small, grassy clearing and enters a forest of tulip poplar, yellow birch, oak, hickory, and an occasional Fraser magnolia. About 0.4 mile from the trailhead, the trail makes the first of four creek crossings. These crossings can be difficult when the water is high. Just beyond this first crossing, cliffs on the right tower above the trail. After the second creek crossing, a significant amount of downfall clogs the route for about 0.5 mile. After the third crossing, the Roaring Fork becomes a series of small falls, ledges, and water slides. Just past the fourth crossing, about 1.4 miles from the trailhead, the trail enters a small clearing.

In the clearing, watch for a road branching to the right. This is the leg back to the trailhead, but first, continue another 0.2 mile up the Roaring Fork to where Cove Branch empties into it. A small waterfall marks this confluence.

Return to the clearing, and take the old road east and south as it weaves in and out of the small bowls and shoulders leading up to Chestnut Ridge. About 1.6 miles from the clearing, the road reaches the ridge crest and crosses another old road. A left here leads to the Appalachian Trail. Instead, turn right and descend the ridge.

This old road is grassy, although some downfall crosses it in places. A forest of small mixed hardwoods dominates the ridge. After 0.9 mile, the trail meets the access road. If you parked at the Roaring Fork ford, turn right on the access road and hike 0.1 mile back to the trailhead. If you left your car at FR 222, turn left and walk 1.2 miles south to end the loop.

Overnight Backpack

Garden Mountain Bushwhack

Distance: 8.2 miles round-trip.
Difficulty: Strenuous.
Topo map: Hutchinson Rock-VA.

HOW TO GET THERE: From the intersection of Interstates 77 and 81 near Wytheville, drive about 10 miles north on I–77 to exit 52. At the stop sign turn left (west) on US 52/Virginia Highway 42. Drive 4.2 miles west and turn right on VA 42. Continue 10.2 miles and turn right on County Road 625. This road forks in 0.4 mile; take the right-hand fork. Drive 7.6 miles north and west (CR 625 turns into Forest Road 222) and turn right onto Forest Road 631. This rough road requires a high-clearance vehicle. Drive 2.6 miles up the mountain to the earthen barrier and trailhead.

This is not a hike for beginners. Expect a significant amount of bushwhacking, and plan to test your compass and topo map skills. The likelihood of solitude is more than enough reward for the challenges this hike presents. The trail begins on an old road that leads gradually down through a forest of oak and hickory down to the Roaring Fork. Nearer the creek, tulip poplar,

A view of Burkes Garden.

hemlock, and Fraser magnolia form the canopy. About 1.7 miles from the trailhead, the trail enters a small clearing and meets an old road that parallels the Roaring Fork.

Turn right here and follow the Roaring Fork a short distance upstream. Walk past the confluence of the Roaring Fork and Cove Branch coming in from the left (west). A small waterfall marks the confluence. At any point beyond this junction, cross the Roaring Fork and begin climbing the ridge. There is no trail, but the way is clear—just aim uphill. The slope is very steep, so take it slow and easy.

After about 1.4 miles, near the lower crest, the mountain begins to flatten out. Red spruce begin to appear in the forest just before you reach the first plateau, which is not the true peak. Once on the ridge crest, hike in a northeasterly direction. The ridge loses elevation slightly as it dips to a small saddle. Cross the saddle and walk toward the left of the tremendous rhododendron thickets ahead. You will have to cross these thickets to reach the summit of Garden Mountain. There is a trail through them, but the opening is difficult to find. Stay to the left of the thickets, gaining elevation, and watch for a small fire pit and campsite near the opening in the rhododendron, about 0.8 mile from where you first reached the ridge crest.

Take the trail through the thicket as it nears the summit of Garden Mountain. On the other side of the rhododendron is a trail junction. A right leads to the 4,710-foot summit of Garden Mountain, which is covered with tall meadow grasses and surrounded by red spruce. Views to the south and east overlook Thompson Valley, Clinch Mountain, and Walker Mountain. The clearing is a great place to camp, and there is water nearby.

Day Hike

Chestnut Ridge

Distance: 7.3 miles round-trip.
Difficulty: Moderate.
Topo map: Hutchinson Rock-VA.

HOW TO GET THERE: The trailhead is the same as for the Garden Mountain Bushwhack.

Cross the earthen barrier and walk 0.1 mile to a junction with an old road that crosses the trail. At this intersection, turn right and begin walking up the ridge, climbing continuously. There are many trees lying across the trail; at times the hiking can be difficult. Quite suddenly, the woods give way to a beautiful meadow with a panoramic view. Shortly after entering the meadow, the trail intersects with the Appalachian Trail, about 1 mile from the trailhead. Turn right and continue climbing the ridge on the AT. Within about 0.5 mile, the trail skirts a pond on the left.

The AT crosses an old fence line and enters the woods. About 3.4 miles from the trailhead, an old road crosses the AT, and there is another small pond on the left. Stay on the AT as it climbs again and enters a clearing on the summit of Chestnut Ridge at an elevation of 4,408 feet. A Beartown Wilderness sign and the Chestnut Knob Shelter share the summit. Enjoy the spectacular view into Burkes Garden to the northeast, and then retrace your tracks to the trailhead.

Lewis Fork Wilderness

Location: 12 miles south of Marion, Virginia.
Size: 6,730 acres.
Administration: USDAFS Jefferson National Forest, Mount Rogers National Recreation Area.
Management status: 5,730-acre wilderness and 1,000-acre nonwilderness roadless area.
Ecosystems: Spruce-fir forest, eastern deciduous forest, and upland meadows.
Elevation range: 3,200 to 5,729 feet.
System trails: 32.8 miles.
Maximum core-to-perimeter distance: 2 miles.
Activities: Hiking, backpacking, and horseback riding.
Modes of travel: Foot and horse.
Maps: Mount Rogers National Recreation Area map; Troutdale-VA and Whitetop Mountain-VA 1:24,000 topo maps.

OVERVIEW: Mount Rogers National Recreation Area is one of the premier hiking destinations in the mid-Atlantic. The area sees visitors from all over the East Coast who want to hike the upland meadows, the Appalachian Trail, and the highest point in Virginia. Amid all of the traffic and attention, wildness prevails in the 5,730 acres of Lewis Fork Wilderness. The wilderness is home to spruce-fir forests, rhododendrons that bloom bright in late June, and fern-covered forest floors.

Thirty miles of trails within the wilderness spread out in all directions. Trails hike steeply up hills, lazily over meadows, and meditatively beside streams. The AT travels through the area, and there are two trail shelters located just outside the wilderness boundaries.

Among all of the highlights of the area, there are two that shine brightest: the meadows of Grayson Highlands and the summit of Mount Rogers. Although technically outside of the wilderness boundary, the upland meadows of Grayson Highlands add a beautiful contrast to the wooded slopes of Lewis Fork. The meadows are alive with wild ponies, deer, and an occasional bear. Late June is ablaze with rhododendron blossoms, and mountain ash and chokecherry also compete for space. The meadows are renowned throughout Virginia; many hikers make this area a weekend destination. If solitude is what you're after, this area is best hiked on a weekday or in the winter. Winter can be especially beautiful, as snowfall transforms the meadows into a pure white wonderland.

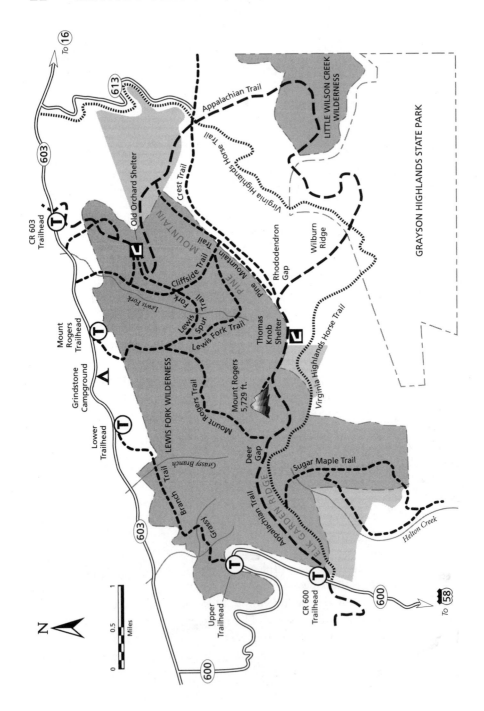

Mount Rogers, the highest peak in Virginia, rises to 5,729 feet between the spines of Pine Mountain and Balsam Mountain, capturing the attention of virtually every Virginia hiker at one time or another. The summit is interesting if not picturesque; there is no view from the top of this peak. The altitude, however, propagates the growth of a spruce-fir forest, giving hikers the opportunity to hike through an environment very rare along Virginia trails.

With plenty of primitive and developed campsites in and around the wilderness, Lewis Fork is a great place to visit. Lower elevations have plenty of water, and there is even a spring on the ridge top along the way to the summit of Mount Rogers. For a wilderness area, Lewis Fork is very hospitable to visitors.

Nevertheless, any wilderness harbors a few dangers to consider when hiking, and Lewis Fork is no different. Most of the wilderness lies above 4,000 feet. At these elevations it is best to be prepared. Weather can change quickly and dramatically. Bring warm clothing and rain gear, and always carry an extra layer of clothing to ward off chills. Also be aware that Lewis Fork is a favored hunting area. When hiking in the fall or early winter, blaze orange should be worn. The two-week rifle season for white-tailed deer is especially dangerous.

RECREATIONAL USES: Mount Rogers National Recreation Area is enjoyed by many outdoor enthusiasts. The AT brings scores of through-hikers across the upland meadows each year around May. Shelters will be full, but the company will be good. Campsites are located at Grindstone Campground on the north side of the wilderness and in Grayson Highlands State Park to the south. These campgrounds bring out scores of day hikers, especially along the shorter trails. The Virginia Highlands Horse Trail is popular among riders, with spring and fall being the most popular seasons. The Helton Creek Trail in the southwestern portion of the wilderness is one of the area's least-used trails.

Day Hike

Grassy Branch Trail

Distance: 3 miles one way.
Difficulty: Easy.
Topo map: Whitetop Mountain-VA.

HOW TO GET THERE: *Lower Trailhead*—From Interstate 81 at Marion, take exit 45 and drive 17.2 miles south on Virginia Highway 16. Turn right on County Road 603 and drive 6.9 miles west to a small parking lot on the right. The trailhead is on the left.

Upper Trailhead—From the lower trailhead, drive another 2.5 miles west and turn left (south) on CR 600. After 100 yards CR 600 turns left again. Continue 3.9 miles south to a parking lot and trailhead on the left.

Grassy Branch is an easy hike through the northwestern corner of Lewis Fork Wilderness. Beginning at the lower trailhead on CR 603, the trail is easy to follow and is dotted with frequent blue blazes. It passes lazily through the woods and dips into several watersheds. The thick canopy creates cool shade on even the hottest summer days. After 3 miles, the trail ends on CR 600 at the upper trailhead. You could leave a shuttle vehicle here, but the hike is easy enough to make a nice out-and-back.

Day Hike

Mount Rogers Summit

Distance: 12.8 miles round-trip.
Difficulty: Strenuous.
Topo map: Whitetop Mountain-VA.

HOW TO GET THERE: From Interstate 81 at Marion, take exit 45 and drive 17.2 miles south on Virginia Highway 16. Turn right on County Road 603 and drive 5.7 miles to a parking lot on the right. The trailhead is on the left side of the road.

As the highest point in Virginia, Mount Rogers draws thousands of hikers eager to climb its flanks. The trail is steady and deliberate, climbing through mixed deciduous forests, a high mountain meadow, and finally, stands of Fraser fir, reason enough to hike this wonderful trail. Do not, however, hike it for a summit view. There isn't one. Views of Briar Ridge and Wilburn Ridge can be enjoyed from the Appalachian Trail just south of the summit.

The trail begins on the south side of CR 603 just past the parking area. A sign marks the trail, and a boardwalk leads into the woods. The trail is blazed blue and is easy to follow as it begins to climb through switchbacks. At about 2.5 miles, the Mount Rogers Trail intersects the Lewis Fork Spur Trail; stay to the right. The trail continues to gain elevation as it passes through stands of hardwoods, into hemlock, and back to hardwood. The angle becomes moderate and the trail begins to wrap around the western flank of the mountain. At 4.8 miles the Mount Rogers Trail reaches the AT. Near this intersection the Tennessee Valley Divide is crossed, marking the separation of streams draining to the Mississippi River and those headed east to the Atlantic Ocean.

At the AT, turn left and continue climbing. Blazes are now white. The AT travels to the edge of a high mountain meadow and turns left near a wooden fence. The Virginia Highlands Trail can be seen crossing the meadow near some boulders. The AT passes a campsite near a stand of red spruce and travels through a few drainage areas that can provide water to the thirsty. Enter

High mountain meadow in Grayson Highlands.

the meadow, and within five minutes of walking, you'll reach the Mount Rogers Spur Trail. A backpacker caught late in the day can continue on the AT to the Thomas Knob Shelter located a few minutes ahead, just across the wilderness border.

Take a left onto the spur trail and climb the last stretch. The meadow is left behind in favor of Fraser fir and red spruce. The highest elevations are the only habitats in Virginia suitable for sustaining these tree species. The understory, composed of moss and fern, is a classic example of boreal forest. A small sign marks the summit, and boulders offer hikers a place to sit.

The hike back to the parking area can be completed in many ways. The obvious route is back the way you came. Another option is to follow the AT to Rhododendron Gap. Enjoy the wonderful views from the rocks above the gap, then go left and follow the blue blazed trail along the crest of Pine Mountain. This trail leads to the Cliffside Trail, which drops back into the wilderness. Follow the Cliffside Trail to the edge of the meadow where the Lewis Fork Trail splits off to the left. The Lewis Fork Trail is a rugged trail that drops to the Lewis Fork Spur Trail, which in turn leads to the Mount Rogers Trail, about 2.5 miles from CR 603. This circuit is long and difficult, but rewards hikers with wonderful views of the surrounding area. The hike back in this direction is about 7.8 miles.

A view of the high balds from Scales Trail between Lewis Fork and Little Wilson Creek Wilderness.

see p. 122

Backpack

Lewis Fork Ramble

Distance: 18.3 miles.
Difficulty: Moderate.
Topo maps: Troutdale-VA and Whitetop Mountain-VA.

HOW TO GET THERE: From Interstate 81 at Marion, take exit 45 and drive 17.2 miles south on Virginia Highway 16. Turn right on County Road 603, drive 9.4 miles, and turn left on CR 600. After 100 yards, CR 600 turns left again. Drive 5.3 miles to the top of the mountain. The parking lot is on the right. The Appalachian Trail crosses the road here.

This is a long hike that pieces together several trails in Lewis Fork to create a loop. The circuit travels through the highlights of the wilderness and boasts two shelters along the way. Old Orchard Shelter is at about the midway point of the hike and is located in an overgrown apple orchard leftover from an old homestead. Thomas Knob Shelter, near the Mount Rogers Spur Trail, has great views of the upland meadow. Both shelters offer overnights in interesting surroundings and are a great way to split a long hike up into shorter sections.

Begin by crossing to the east side of the road and walking up the AT. The Appalachian Trail in this area, as well as many of the side trails, is maintained by volunteers in the Mount Rogers Appalachian Trail Club.

The trail starts at a meadow just off CR 600 and makes a steady climb along Elk Garden Ridge to Deep Gap. The AT crosses a gate before entering the wilderness, then begins the moderate climb. Watch for a rock outcrop on the right with views to the southwest. Deep Gap is a former trail-shelter site. Overuse, however, put a strain on the environment, and camping in this area is no longer permitted. The Virginia Highlands Trail also passes through the gap just south of the AT.

From Deep Gap, the AT climbs slightly and then contours south around the peak of Mount Rogers. The Mount Rogers Trail is passed as the AT moves out of Deep Gap. This is the trail that you will return on near the end of the loop. As the AT travels around the south side of Mount Rogers, the forest type changes dramatically from hardwoods to spruce and yellow birch and finally to upland meadow. The AT comes to a fence where there are beautiful views of the meadow. The trail skirts a spring and then enters the meadow. Pass the Mount Rogers Spur Trail on the left (or follow it for a 0.5-mile detour to the state's highest point).

Soon the AT reaches Thomas Knob Shelter. There is a privy at the shelter, and the area appears to see much use. The AT climbs briefly after the shelter, and then drops to Rhododendron Gap, about 5.3 miles from the trailhead. Several trails converge in this gap; a signpost gives directions. Turn left here onto Pine Mountain Trail. (If you stay on the AT and skip the Pine Mountain Trail shortcut, the hike would be about 18 miles one way and would pass through nearby Little Wilson Creek Wilderness.) The trail branches again and the Crest Trail moves off to the right. Stay left and follow the blue-blazed old route of the AT on the ridge crest.

The hike along Pine Mountain is picturesque. Rock outcrops give views of the meadow and the valleys below. After 1.8 miles the trail intersects with the current AT. Turn left onto the AT and start the hike down into Lewis Fork.

As the AT loses elevation, the meadows are left behind. The trail turns rocky and enters a boggy forest of ferns. There are many springs in this area, and the forest changes from higher-elevation spruce-fir forests to lower-elevation mixed hardwoods. The AT reenters Lewis Fork at about 7.8 miles, and at about 8.5 miles reaches the Old Orchard Shelter.

Another wonderful place to overnight, the Old Orchard Shelter is situated in a beautiful meadow surrounded by apple trees and large, shady sugar maples. There is a picnic table at the shelter, and water is available as well. This shelter is located about 1.5 miles from the AT parking area on CR 603. If a car were left at this parking lot, the one-way hike would be about 10 miles.

To continue the hike, follow the AT past the shelter and turn left on Old Orchard Trail, which climbs uphill to meet the Lewis Fork Spur Trail. The easy-to-moderate grade travels through forests of mixed hardwoods. Continue straight past the junction with the Cliffside Trail.

Follow Lewis Fork Spur through the drainage of the stream. The trail passes the junction of the Lewis Fork Trail before it reaches the Mount Rogers Trail. There are nice campsites at the junction with the Mount Rogers Trail, but no water is available. Take a left on the Mount Rogers Trail and follow it up the ridge to the junction with the AT (for more details on the Mount Rogers Trail, see the description earlier in this chapter). Turn right (west) on the AT and cruise down Elk Garden Ridge to your vehicle on CR 600.

Little Wilson Creek Wilderness

Location: 11 miles south of Marion, Virginia.
Size: 5,678 acres.
Administration: USDAFS Jefferson National Forest, Mount Rogers National Recreation Area.
Management status: 3,900-acre wilderness and 1,778-acre nonwilderness roadless area.
Ecosystems: Spruce-fir forest, oak-hickory forest, and upland meadows.
Elevation range: 3,200 to 4,857 feet.
System trails: 22.6 miles.
Maximum core-to-perimeter distance: 1.8 miles.
Activities: Hiking, backpacking, and horseback riding.
Modes of travel: Foot and horse.
Maps: Mount Rogers National Recreation Area map; Troutdale-VA 1:24,000 topo map.

OVERVIEW: The Little Wilson Creek area is a small package bursting at the seams with wilderness qualities. It boasts some of the highest peaks in Virginia, topping out at 4,857-foot Second Peak. The slopes fall away to beautiful cascading trout streams and oak-hickory forests where Virginia northern flying squirrels make their homes. Trails traverse the area in all directions. Despite its 3,900-acre size, this wilderness feels much, much bigger.

Most of the area lies above 4,000 feet, and large grassy balds contrast sharply with the forests below. One particularly large bald can be reached via the Bearpen Trail. The forests here are diverse, and the mix of trees varies depending on elevation, moisture, and slope aspect. South-facing slopes are drier, while north-facing slopes and damp pockets harbor large Fraser magnolia, yellow birch, and other water-loving species. Red spruce and Fraser fir thrive at higher elevations.

The trail system includes 25 miles of well-marked routes within the area and along its perimeter. Water is available from the many streams and springs. Most of the trails are in excellent condition; many are open to both foot and horse travel. The hiking is easy and the trails appear to be well used but not overcrowded. If solitude is your goal, the Hightree Rock Trail sees the fewest number of visitors. Areas of interest in the wilderness include a beautiful boulder-strewn meadow on the Bearpen Trail. The First Peak Trail offers many panoramic views, and the Little Wilson Creek Trail is a beautiful streamside trail.

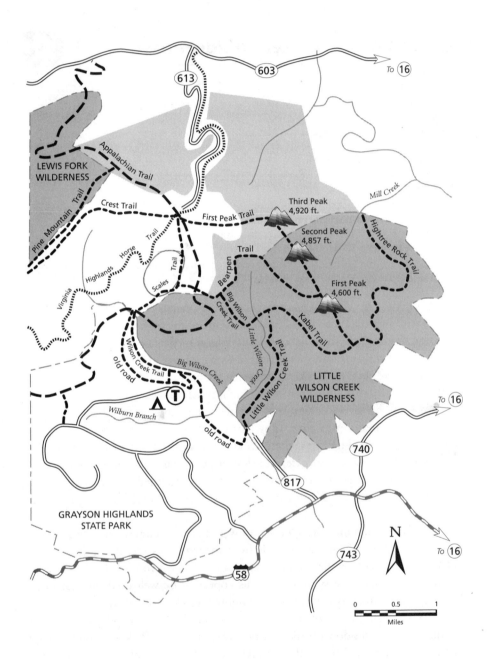

To (16)

603

613

LEWIS FORK
WILDERNESS

Appalachian Trail

Pine Mountain Trail

Crest Trail

Trail

Horse

Highlands

Virginia

Scales Trail

First Peak Trail

Mill Creek

Third Peak
4,920 ft.

Second Peak
4,857 ft.

First Peak
4,600 ft.

Bearpen Trail

Hightree Rock Trail

Big Wilson Creek Trail

Kabel Trail

LITTLE
WILSON CREEK
WILDERNESS

Wilson Creek Trail

old road

Big Wilson Creek

Little Wilson Creek

Little Wilson Creek Trail

Wilburn Branch

old road

740

817

To (16)

GRAYSON HIGHLANDS
STATE PARK

58

743

To (16)

N

0   0.5   1
Miles

If you finally run out of things to see in Little Wilson Creek, you don't have far to go for more of Virginia's wonderful outdoors. Little Wilson Creek is part of Mount Rogers National Recreation Area. The peak of Mount Rogers is in the Lewis Fork Wilderness, accessible via the Appalachian Trail, which skirts Little Wilson Creek's western boundary. Grayson Highlands State Park borders Little Wilson Creek to the south. This popular, full-featured state park offers numerous campsites and also contains the trailheads for many of the trails through Little Wilson Creek.

RECREATIONAL USES: With the proximity of Grayson Highlands State Park and Mount Rogers National Recreation Area, Little Wilson Creek sees many visitor days of hiking each year. People come from all over the East Coast to hike and backpack in this upland portion of Virginia. Of the backcountry hikes, Bearpen and First Peak Trails get the most use. Wilson Creek Trail is a favorite day hike for many visitors. Horseback riding is also very popular. Horse trails and fire roads are scattered throughout the highlands, and many trails in Little Wilson Creek allow horse travel. Trout fishing can be good in Wilson Creek, and hunters roam the area during the various game seasons. There seems to be very little the outdoorsperson cannot do in Little Wilson Creek or its neighboring areas.

Day Hike

Wilson Creek Trail

Distance: 2.8 miles round-trip.
Difficulty: Easy.
Topo map: Troutdale-VA.

HOW TO GET THERE: The best way to access the Little Wilson Creek area is from Grayson Highlands State Park. From Interstate 81 in Marion, take exit 45 and turn south on Virginia Highway 16. Drive 23 miles south and turn west (right) on US 58. Continue 7.6 miles west to the park entrance on the right. Follow the signs for the campground to get to the trailheads. Look for a sign for the trail with parking on the left side of the road near the campground store. There is a small fee to enter the park.

Wilson Creek Trail is an excellent walk for relieving stress or for digesting a picnic lunch on Sunday afternoon. The trail is a short, scenic walk along the boundary between Grayson Highlands State Park and the Little Wilson Creek Wilderness. The stream is loud and swift as it flows over boulders and tumbles down waterfalls.

From the trailhead, the trail crosses a dirt road and drops sharply to the creek. Turn left and follow the creek, gaining little elevation. The hike is pleasant and easy. There is an interesting stand of Fraser magnolia along the way. When the trail begins a short, steep climb along a dirt road the end is near. A left on the road leads back to the trailhead.

Day Hike

Little Wilson Creek Trail

Distance: 6 miles round-trip.
Difficulty: Moderate.
Topo map: Troutdale-VA.

HOW TO GET THERE: See the directions to the Wilson Creek Trailhead in Grayson Highlands State Park.

Little Wilson Creek Trail is one of the lesser-used trails in the wilderness area. This is not due to it being particularly strenuous; in fact the hiking is easy to moderate. But access to the trail is a little difficult. From within the wilderness, the only access is via a short bushwhack off the Kabel Trail. (Access to the trail from CR 817 is interrupted by a stretch of private property. Trail users should not attempt to access the trail from CR 817.) From Grayson Highlands State Park, the trailhead lies across the creek at the end of a 2.3-mile hike along an old fire road. These minor inconveniences should not deter one from hiking this wonderful trail. Little Wilson Creek is a delightful stream to explore.

The hike begins at the campground in Grayson Highlands State Park. Follow the old road down the ridge and turn southeast. The road contours until it reaches a power line. Turn left at the power line and travel downhill to the creek. There is an old apple orchard here. Cross the creek and follow a small trail up the bank to the Little Wilson Creek Trail. Turn left and hike uphill. A sign marks the entrance to the wilderness.

From the wilderness boundary, the trail travels easily uphill through rocks and large boulders, following the stream toward its beginning. The trail flirts with the stream, sometimes coming down to the water, sometimes leaving the stream far below. The banks are shaded by large hemlocks, some of which have fallen across the deeper ravines. Laurel completes the understory; it blooms in June and makes hikes during this time of year particularly spectacular.

True to the maps, the trail begins to die out. From this point there are two options. The first and most obvious is to turn back and complete the hike as an out-and-back. The second is to bushwhack 0.8 mile to the Kabel Trail and hike other trails back to the parking area. The bushwhack is not extremely difficult, although it does travel through a laurel thicket. Getting through the thicket requires agility and patience, and at times even crawling on hands and knees. Stay on the right side of the creek and follow it upstream. When you reach a small meadow, the intersection with the Kabel Trail is near.

From the Kabel Trail there are more options. A right leads to First Peak Trail and Hightree Rock Trail, the least-used trail in the wilderness. Those seeking solitude should choose this trail, although it is an out-and-back. A left at the intersection with the Kabel Trail leads to Big Wilson Creek Trail. From there, you can hike along the Bearpen and Scales Trails back to Grayson Highlands and the trailhead (see the First Peak day hike description below).

Day Hike

First Peak Loop

Distance: 10.2 miles.
Difficulty: Moderate.
Topo map: Troutdale-VA.

HOW TO GET THERE: Follow the directions for the Wilson Creek Trail.

The First Peak Loop links many short trails in Little Wilson Creek to create a fairly long hike through the core of the wilderness. The highlights of the hike are First Peak and Second Peak, both of which reach almost 5,000 feet in elevation.

The trails are well maintained and easy to follow. Begin by walking northwest on Wilson Creek Trail along the creek to the end at a dirt road. This is the beginning of the Scales Trail. Turn right and follow the Scales Trail up the ridge, enjoying views of Pine Mountain and the surrounding meadows. The Scales Trail intersects first with the Appalachian Trail and then the Bearpen Trail. Turn right onto the Bearpen Trail, which skirts a spring and then traverses a grassy bald.

The 1.7-mile Bearpen Trail travels along the northern boundary of the wilderness before ending in a saddle between First and Second Peaks. The Bearpen Trail is easy and follows gentle contours for most of its length, passing intersections with the AT and Big Wilson Creek Trail. Near the intersection with Big Wilson Creek Trail, the Bearpen Trail passes several small springs that produce enough moisture to support a stand of yellow birch.

At the intersection with the First Peak Trail, you are in Virginia's high country. Turn left and hike 0.6 mile to the crest of Second Peak, which tops out at 4,857 feet. Turn around and hike back into the saddle and continue southeast toward First Peak. The trail climbs quickly to this 4,600-foot peak and then drops gradually to the junction with the Kabel and Hightree Rock Trails.

Turn right onto the Kabel Trail. After climbing the peaks, the easy grade of the Kabel Trail is a welcome rest. The trail crosses several wet areas, which could be quite muddy. Follow the trail around the ridge. After about 1.5 miles, watch for the trail to make an abrupt left turn down a steep ridge. The trail has been following an old road grade, which continues to contour as the trail turns left. It is easy to miss this turn. Follow the trail down a short steep section to a small meadow and the headwaters of Little Wilson Creek. Continue 0.5 mile to the intersection with Big Wilson Creek Trail. A left at this intersection leads downhill and the trail runs out.

Follow the Big Wilson Creek Trail, which exits to the right at a small sign and begins to climb. The trail is difficult in spots as it makes its way back to the Bearpen Trail. At the Bearpen Trail, take a left, hike a short distance, and then take another left onto the section of the AT that you passed on the hike in. As usual, the AT is well marked and easy to follow. This 1.3-mile section travels steeply downhill, contours, and then bends northwest to travel uphill to the intersection with the Scales Trail. Hiking the Bearpen Trail back to the Scales Trail is probably a little easier, but it's hard to pass up any miles on the magnificent AT.

Back on the Scales Trail, turn left and coast back to the trailhead. At the dirt road on the Grayson Highlands side of Wilson Creek, you can hike the road or Wilson Creek Trail to return to the trailhead; the dirt road is more direct. Wilson Creek Trail is more scenic, but leaves a long climb for the end of the day.

Little Dry Run Wilderness

Location: 13 miles southwest of Wytheville, Virginia.
Size: 6,902 acres.
Administration: USDAFS Jefferson National Forest, Mount Rogers National Recreation Area.
Management status: 3,400-acre wilderness and a 3,502-acre nonwilderness roadless area.
Ecosystems: Eastern deciduous forest.
Elevation range: 2,800 to 3,614 feet.
System trails: 13.3 miles.
Maximum core-to-perimeter distance: 1.5 miles.
Activities: Hiking, backpacking, and horseback riding.
Modes of travel: Foot and horse.
Maps: Mount Rogers National Recreation Area map; Cedar Springs-VA and Speedwell-VA 1:24,000 topo maps.

OVERVIEW: The Little Dry Run is a small wilderness tucked away on a shoulder of Iron Mountain. While hikers in southwestern Virginia congregate and crowd into Mount Rogers National Recreation Area, nearby Little Dry Run remains relatively unnoticed. The main hiking trail is wonderfully lonely as it meanders along the cool and shady banks of the run.

The characteristics of this wilderness make it perfect for day hiking or a weekend trip. First, the area is small—most of it can be seen in a day or two. The two trails in the area, Little Dry Run Trail and the Virginia Highlands Trail, are relatively short and can be linked into a makeshift loop hike. Second, access to the area is easy, with parking either right on US 21 or not far from it. Third, overnight campers are rewarded with easily attainable campsites. Primitive camping with nearby water sources can be found throughout the wilderness. Car campers can stay at Comers Rock Campground, located near the upper trailhead for Little Dry Run Trail.

RECREATIONAL USES: Little Dry Run is a small wilderness but is similar to the other larger Virginia wilderness lands in its usage. There is a significant amount of hunting during the game seasons. Be aware and check the local regulations when hiking in the fall and early winter. Hiking is popular in the wilderness. Comers Rock Campground allows for car camping and easy access to the interior wilderness. The Virginia Highlands Trail does distinguish Little

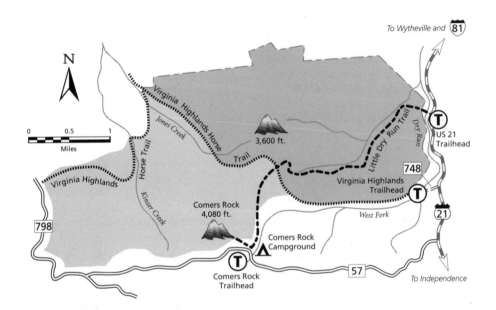

Dry Run from many other Virginia wilderness areas. This trail is designed for horse travel and traverses almost the entire length of Mount Rogers National Recreation Area. The trail is wide, camping areas are spacious, and the parking lot at the trailhead is large enough for horse trailers.

Day Hike

Little Dry Run Trail

Distance: 3.9 miles one way.
Difficulty: Moderate.
Topo map: Speedwell-VA.

HOW TO GET THERE: *US 21 Trailhead*—From Interstate 81 at Wytheville, take exit 70 and drive south 15.6 miles on US 21. The trailhead is on the right (west) and parking is on the left (east).

Comers Rock Trailhead—From the US 21 Trailhead, continue 2.3 miles to Forest Road 57. Turn right and drive 2 miles west to Comers Rock Campground. The trail starts here and heads north.

On a hot summer day, streamside trails are a hiker's delight. Down beside the stream, the tree canopy is thicker, the shade is darker, and the sweet summer air is cooler. Little Dry Run is just such a trail, once it drops down the ridge from Comers Rock Campground to Little Dry Run and US 21. The trail begins at 4,000 feet and descends to 2,485 feet.

The trail begins at the northwestern end of Comers Rock Campground. Find the sign for the Iron Mountain Trail and follow this path to another sign with directions to Comers Rock and the West Fork of Dry Run. At this juncture, you'll turn right toward Little Dry Run, but before you take off down the trail, it is worth it to hike up to Comers Rock west of the trailhead. The walk is short and the views are good.

The first part of Little Dry Run Trail is through oak-hickory forest as it descends the ridge to the wilderness boundary. The trail first descends rapidly, bending through a gully that eventually forms the run. The trail continues to drop quickly off the ridge, then levels out and contours across a finger ridge. The next section descends to the intersection with the Virginia Highlands Trail about 1.3 miles from Comers Rock Campground. A trail register marks this intersection.

Continue down Little Dry Run Trail as it drops steeply down a band of rocks and then bends left and levels out. From this point on, the trail follows Little Dry Run to US 21. The forest changes to hemlock and rhododendron. Intermittent yellow blazes mark the trail, but the route can be less apparent on several "blazeless" stretches. When in doubt, follow the stream and the trail will reappear. Eventually, the trail widens and travels through beautiful stands of hemlock growing among large boulders.

There is one more landmark you should watch for. About 2.5 miles from the Virginia Highlands Trail, the Little Dry Run Trail branches right and up-hill while another trail stays straight. This other trail leads out of the wilderness to private property. The Little Dry Run Trail wraps around the ridge and then, with a left switchback, leads down to Dry Run. The trail crosses the stream and heads out to US 21. A parking lot and Forest Service information stand are across the road.

The Little Dry Run Trail can be made into a loop hike by linking with the Virginia Highlands Trail. To do this, walk about 0.9 mile south on the shoulder of US 21 and turn right (west) onto FR 748. Walk 0.6 mile up this road to the trailhead for the Virginia Highlands Trail. Follow the Virginia Highlands Trail west along the West Fork to the intersection with the Little Dry Run Trail. Turn left and follow the Little Dry Run Trail south and up the ridge to the Comers Rock Campground where you started. Alternatively, the circuit can start at the Virginia Highlands Trailhead. Park here; hike up the trail, down the Dry Run Trail, and then follow US 21 back to the trailhead.

Day Hike or Horseback Ride

Virginia Highlands Horse Trail

Distance: 9.6 miles round-trip.
Difficulty: Moderate.
Topo map: Speedwell-VA.

HOW TO GET THERE: From Interstate 81 at Wytheville, take exit 70 and drive south 16.8 miles on US 21. Turn right on Forest Road 748 and go 0.6 mile to the trailhead and parking lot.

The Virginia Highlands Horse Trail is a long and popular trail in southwest Virginia. In high horse-traffic areas such as Mount Rogers, hiking this trail is not recommended. It can be muddy and rutted and generally an unpleasant walk. The section of trail in the Little Dry Run Wilderness, however, is less popular with horse riders, and can be enjoyed by riders and hikers alike.

The wide, easy-to-follow trail begins at the trailhead on FR 748 off of US 21. The first section of the trail climbs gradually as the forest changes from hemlock and cove hardwoods to oak, hickory, and maple. There are views of the Little Dry Run Valley along the way. The trail climbs to a saddle where it meets with the Little Dry Run Trail.

From the intersection, the trail slowly drops into the Jones Creek drainage and follows the stream down the valley. There are several stream crossings, and several side trails and roads are passed; stay on the main route. After the last stream crossing, the trail begins to climb out of the valley. It is at this point that the Virginia Highlands Trail leaves the wilderness behind. Turn around here and make your way back to the trailhead.

North Creek Roadless Area

Location: 7 miles east of Buchanan, Virginia.
Size: 4,955 acres.
Administration: USDAFS Jefferson National Forest, Glenwood Ranger District.
Management status: Nonwilderness roadless area.
Ecosystems: Eastern deciduous forest.
Elevation range: 1,475 to 3,320 feet.
System trails: 15 miles.
Maximum core-to-perimeter distance: 2.5 miles.
Activities: Hiking.
Modes of travel: Foot.
Maps: Glenwood Ranger District map; Arnold Valley-VA and Peaks of Otter-VA 1:24,000 topo maps.

OVERVIEW: The North Creek roadless area lies on the western ridge of the Blue Ridge Mountains. The area encompasses all of Backbone Ridge and Floyd Mountain and also protects the watershed of the upper reaches of North Creek and Cornelius Creek. Gentle slopes and quiet flowing creeks mark the western region of the roadless area. Steep ridges climbing to the crest of the Blue Ridge characterize the eastern portion.

The jewel of the North Creek area is the Apple Orchard Falls Special Management Area. The area was given special management status to protect the scenic beauty of the falls, which make a sheer 200-foot drop. Towering cliffs mark the entrance to the falls from both directions. Below the falls, the creek is strewn with large boulders. The spectacular beauty of Apple Orchard Falls attracts numerous visitors all year long.

Several species of oak and hickory dominate the area's overstory, while dogwood, serviceberry, and mountain laurel are found in the understory. In the sheltered creek bottoms, tall cove hardwoods are found in abundance. Hemlock and white pine can also be found in these areas. The region is also home to the rare Peaks of Otter salamander.

The National Forest Service has determined that a 7-mile segment of North Creek is eligible for designation as a Wild and Scenic River. The lower stretch of the creek is a popular stocked trout stream, while the upper stretch is a high-quality trout stream. The headwaters of both North Creek and Cornelius Creek are important native trout fisheries.

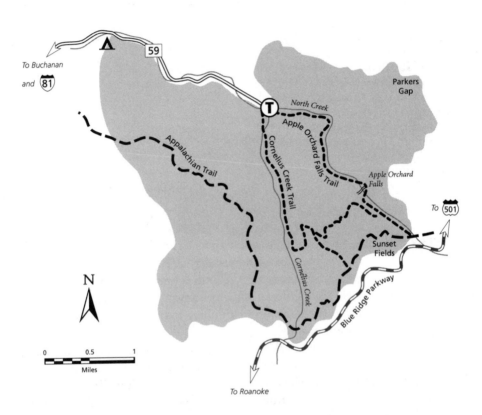

To Buchanan
and 81

59

Parkers
Gap

T   North Creek

Apple Orchard Falls Trail

Cornelius Creek Trail

Appalachian Trail

Apple Orchard
Falls

To 501

Sunset
Fields

Cornelius Creek

Blue Ridge Parkway

N

0   0.5   1
Miles

To Roanoke

RECREATIONAL USES: The Apple Orchard Falls Trail is a National Recreational Trail; the major recreational use of this area is hiking. The trail leads to several scenic regions, including the Apple Orchard Falls, which offer a beautiful setting to delight the most avid of outdoor photographers. The Appalachian Trail also winds its way through this roadless area. The 8-mile stretch of AT climbs almost 2,000 feet along the crest of Floyd Mountain. The region is also unusual for its bird population, offering the opportunity to view several species of neotropical migratory songbirds that spend the warmer months in the area of the Apple Orchard Falls. Finally, because both North Creek and Cornelius Creek have populations of native trout, anglers can test their skills in the quiet pools leading up to the falls.

Day Hike

Apple Orchard Falls/Cornelius Creek Loop Trail

Distance: 5.75 miles or 7.0 miles.
Difficulty: Moderate.
Topo map: Arnold Valley-VA.

HOW TO GET THERE: Take Interstate 81 to exit 168. At the stop sign, turn east on County Road 614. Travel 3.3 miles and take a left on Forest Road 59. After 2.8 miles the road changes to gravel. Continue 1.6 miles to the parking area for the trailhead.

The Apple Orchard Falls Trail, marked with blue blazes, begins at a Forest Service information center and a sign designating the Special Management Area. After crossing a wooden bridge, the trail follows an old road, with North Creek on the left. This easy flat stretch is dominated by large cove hardwoods and towering hemlocks. After approximately 0.5 mile, the trail leaves the road and becomes a path.

After the trail exits the road, the climb becomes more strenuous. Large boulders begin to dot the landscape. These boulders mark the entrance to the falls area, and the trail becomes very steep. The 200-foot Apple Orchard Falls tumbles over a high rock face. Upon reaching the falls, the trail crosses the stream via a bridge and continues the steep ascent to huge granite cliffs on the right. Throughout this area are tall straight hemlocks. The difficult steep climb becomes moderate, and the trail reaches the junction of another old road. A left on the road leads to Parkers Gap trailhead, a right leads to the Cornelius Creek Trail. The Apple Orchard Falls Trail continues straight up the mountain, connecting with the Appalachian Trail in 0.6 mile and the Blue Ridge Parkway in 0.8 mile. To hike the longer loop, stay on the Apple Orchard Falls Trail to

The Apple Orchard Falls Trail.

Sunset Fields, turn south at the junction with the AT, and continue to the Cornelius Creek Trail.

For the shorter hike, turn right on the old road. The trees along the road are covered with muscadine grapevines. These grapes are a tasty treat in late fall. The road begins a series of easy ups and downs to the signed junction with the Cornelius Creek Trail. The AT is 0.5 mile uphill; the Cornelius Creek Trail begins a descent to the parking area on FR 59. There is a small clearing at this junction that makes a good spot for camping, but there is no water.

The trailhead is approximately 1.75 miles from this junction. The descent to the creek is steep and rocky. Many of the rocks are loose, making secure footing difficult. After a right switchback, the grade becomes more moderate, but the trail is still rocky. Tree species include oak, hickory, and maple. The trail crosses the creek, and a number of small waterfalls are visible from the trail. After the third creek crossing, the grade becomes easy, the creek is on the right, and the loop is almost complete. Continue north a short distance to the trailhead on FR 59.

Thunder Ridge Wilderness

Location: 16 miles south of Lexington, Virginia.
Size: 2,450 acres.
Administration: USDAFS Jefferson National Forest, Glenwood Ranger District.
Management status: Wilderness area.
Ecosystems: Eastern deciduous forest.
Elevation range: 1,320 to 4,225 feet.
System trails: 6.2 miles of maintained trails.
Maximum core-to-perimeter distance: 1 mile.
Activities: Hiking and horseback riding.
Modes of travel: Foot and horse.
Maps: Glenwood Ranger District map; Arnold Valley-VA, and Snowden-VA 1:24,000 topo maps.

OVERVIEW: Thunder Ridge is a small wilderness located in Rockbridge and Botetourt Counties about 17 miles south of Lexington, Virginia, in Jefferson National Forest. Thunder Ridge occupies an area of 2,450 acres and was declared a wilderness by Congress in 1984.

The wilderness is located on the western slope of the Blue Ridge near Apple Orchard Mountain. The Blue Ridge Parkway forms most of the eastern boundary, and Forest Road 35 forms the northern boundary. The region is rugged and unforgiving. The terrain climbs rapidly from the western boundary on the slope of Thunder Ridge to the crest of the mountain. In some areas, the angle of the slope is close to 70 degrees. The area near the top is very dry, but farther down the ridge, in some cases almost on the western boundary, there are small springs that feed both the East Fork and Elk Creek. Elevations range from 1,320 feet to almost 4,225 feet near the top of Apple Orchard Mountain.

Cove species such as tulip poplar, oak, and hemlock inhabit many of the sheltered regions of the wilderness. Some of these trees are very large. Near the crest of Apple Orchard Mountain, there is an interesting mix of species. Not only are the hardwoods present, such as red and white oak, but common persimmon is also represented in large numbers. Due to the high elevation, small red spruce and yellow birch can also be found. The harsh environment of the dry western slopes supports species such as pitch pine, Virginia pine, and chestnut oak. There are many flowers found in this wilderness area, including

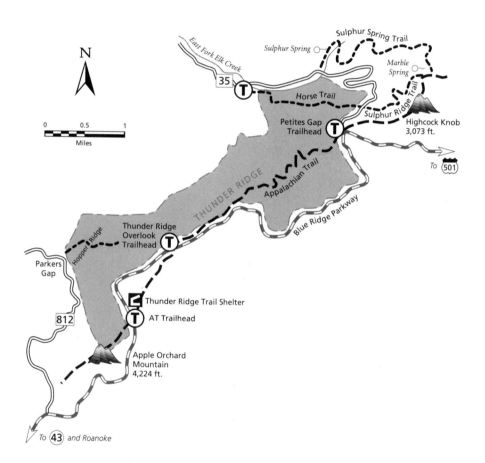

N

0   0.5   1
Miles

East Fork Elk Creek

Sulphur Spring Trail

Sulphur Spring

Marble Spring

35

Horse Trail

Sulphur Ridge Trail

Petites Gap Trailhead

Highcock Knob 3,073 ft.

To 501

THUNDER RIDGE

Appalachian Trail

Blue Ridge Parkway

Thunder Ridge Overlook Trailhead

Hopper Ridge

Parkers Gap

812

Thunder Ridge Trail Shelter

AT Trailhead

Apple Orchard Mountain 4,224 ft.

To 43 and Roanoke

wild columbine, pink lady's slipper, trillium, purple-flowering raspberry, and fire pink. Mountain laurel and rhododendron also thrive here.

RECREATIONAL USES: Few trails traverse this wilderness, due to the rugged nature of the land. The major trail—the Appalachian Trail—lies across the top of the ridge. It travels through Thunder Ridge in two places for a combined total of about 4.3 miles. The only other maintained trail is a horse trail located near FR 35. One other area that offers hiking is near Hopper Ridge, at the southern end of the wilderness. Hopper Ridge is unmaintained and difficult to hike in the summer. Adding it to the 6.2 miles of maintained trail brings the area's total up to about 8 miles.

The AT is the only trail that is heavily used here. The rest of the wilderness sees few visitors. If seeking solitude, the lower half of the wilderness is the place to find it. One note of caution regarding the lower half of the wilderness area: The land fronting the wilderness has been heavily logged, making access difficult. There are, however, ways in.

Day Hike

Appalachian Trail—Thunder Ridge

Distance: 3.3 miles one way.
Difficulty: Easy.
Topo map: Arnold Valley-VA.

HOW TO GET THERE: This hike is short enough to do as an out-and-back, but a car shuttle between the two trailheads will save you the trip back (and up-hill). To set up the shuttle, first leave a car at the Petites Gap Trailhead. From Lynchburg, drive about 20 miles northwest on US 501. Turn left onto the Blue Ridge Parkway and drive south about 9 miles to Forest Road 35 near milepost 71. Turn right (north) onto FR 35 and drive about 0.1 mile to the trailhead and parking lot at Petites Gap. Leave your shuttle car here, then drive back to the Blue Ridge Parkway, turn right, and drive about 3 miles south to the Thunder Ridge Overlook between mileposts 74 and 75.

The trail begins at the north end of the parking lot near the summit of Thunder Ridge. It slowly winds north and downhill along the ridge to Petites Gap, traveling through a forest of mixed hardwoods and occasional thickets of rhododendron. Water is available at only a few places along the trail; remember to pack enough for the trip.

The AT is well marked with white blazes. Before starting the journey, stop at the overlook for an excellent view of Arnold Valley, House Mountain, and the Devil's Marble Yard in the James River Face Wilderness. Hike about 0.5 mile and cross the boundary into the wilderness area. The tops of many of the trees here are broken, and there is a great deal of dead wood lying on the ground.

At 1 mile the AT begins a long gradual climb. A small rocky outcrop on the left provides a good view of the valley. Just beyond the summit of this small ridge is an excellent place to camp, with level ground and a small spring. A large basswood tree grows near the center of this clearing, offering welcome shade. Just beyond the campsite the trail becomes steeper. After a left switchback, the grade moderates and there is a good view of Highcock Knob, also in the James River Face Wilderness.

About 2.5 miles into the hike, the trail crosses a small creek and enters a thicket of rhododendron and mountain laurel, with hemlock and white pine in the overstory. When the trail tops a small shoulder, it begins a final descent to FR 35. There are three switchbacks during this descent. The forest in this region is old growth with some very impressive trees. Near the junction with FR 35, a sign gives the distances to the Thunder Ridge Trail Shelter (4.6 miles) and FR 812 (7 miles).

Day Hike

Appalachian Trail—Apple Orchard Mountain

Distance: 1.6 miles round-trip.
Difficulty: Easy.
Topo map: Arnold Valley-VA.

HOW TO GET THERE: Follow the directions to the Thunder Ridge Overlook on the Blue Ridge Parkway. Continue south on the parkway another 1.5 miles to an Appalachian Trail parking lot and trailhead near milepost 76. The trail begins on the west side of the road.

This short section of the AT climbs from the Blue Ridge Parkway to the 4,224-foot summit of Apple Orchard Mountain. The AT heads south from the parkway, meanders through a short stretch of woods, and enters a small meadow. Red spruce and yellow birch grow along the fringe of this meadow. The AT exits the meadow and begins a short climb to the summit of Apple Orchard Mountain. Just before the summit, the trail passes under a boulder that is wedged between two other boulders. After crossing the wilderness boundary, the trail enters another small meadow. Follow the AT to a short side trail leading to the summit, then retrace your route back to the trailhead.

Day Hike

Horse Trail Loop

Distance: 7.9 miles.
Difficulty: Moderate.
Topo map: Snowden-VA.

HOW TO GET THERE: *From Lexington,* take Interstate 81 south to exit 180. Drive 3.5 miles south on US 11 to Virginia Highway 130. Turn left on VA 130 and drive 3.2 miles east to County Road 759. Turn right on CR 759 and drive 3.2 miles south up the Arnold Valley. Turn left on CR 781 and drive 2.1 miles east to a parking lot on the right. (CR 781 becomes Forest Road 35 in this stretch.)

From Lynchburg, drive about 20 miles north and west on US 501, and turn south on the Blue Ridge Parkway. Drive about 9 miles south on the parkway to FR 35. Turn right and drive about 4 miles down this winding road to the East Fork of Elk Creek. The parking lot and trailhead are on the left (south) side of the road.

This loop travels through both the Thunder Ridge Wilderness and the James River Face Wilderness. Although the trail is maintained for horseback riding, it makes a nice hiking loop as well. The length of the loop can be varied somewhat, depending on the trail selected. The loop begins on a little-used trail on the northern end of the Thunder Ridge Wilderness. The trail is marked with orange blazes. The first section of the loop passes through a forest of tall cove hardwoods, hemlock, and white pine. After crossing the East Fork, the trail climbs at an easy pace away from the creek and then drops to the creek again.

The trail makes a big bend to the right, leaving the East Fork behind, and the climb becomes more moderate. About 0.8 mile from the trailhead, an old road branches right; stay on the left-hand fork. After a series of switchbacks, the trail flattens out for a short distance. At 1.5 miles the trail crosses a creek, but the climb continues. As it climbs out of the creek drainage, the trail passes through a forest of much smaller trees. Coppice growth would indicate that logging occurred in this region not too long ago. Just beyond this growth of small trees, the trail joins FR 35 about 2.1 miles from the trailhead.

Cross the road and enter the James River Face Wilderness. After crossing an earthen barrier, the loop follows the Sulphur Ridge Trail. The grade becomes easy as the trail follows the contours of the mountain along an old road. About 0.5 mile from FR 35, the trail forks. Take the right-hand fork, which reverts to trail and begins to climb. Shortly after this fork, the trail intersects with the Appalachian Trail.

Turn left on the AT and begin a 0.3-mile descent to the Marble Spring region, a flat area in a saddle between Highcock Knob and Piney Ridge. There is a small spring downhill and to the left. From this area the AT climbs steadily to the crest of Piney Ridge, where several trails intersect. A sign with distances marks this intersection, about 4.2 miles from the trailhead.

Take a left on the Sulphur Spring Trail, which is actually a wide old road. It descends at a gradual pace to FR 35, passing through a dry region of the James River Face Wilderness with a small, scrubby forest. Small pitch pine and chestnut oak dominate the overstory, while mountain laurel, blueberry, and huckleberry thrive near the ground.

About 0.9 mile down the ridge, a rock outcrop affords a great view to the south and west. This panoramic view highlights Thunder Ridge. Just before reaching FR 35, the trail bends to the left and crosses Sulphur Spring. Large hemlock, white pine, and tulip poplar grow here, and poison ivy crowds the trail.

At the junction of FR 35, turn right and walk 1 mile along the road back to your car. Be on the lookout for the Blue Hole, a small swimming area on the East Fork. A swinging rope and a small cliff dare thrill seekers. Diving from the rock, however, is not advised.

Location: 14 miles south of Lexington, Virginia.
Size: 8,903 acres.
Administration: USDAFS Jefferson National Forest, Glenwood Ranger District.
Management status: 8,903-acre wilderness and a 1,140-acre roadless area.
Ecosystems: Eastern deciduous forest.
Elevation range: 660 to 3,073 feet.
System trails: 27 miles of maintained trails.
Maximum core-to-perimeter distance: 3.2 miles.
Activities: Horseback riding, hiking, backpacking, and canoeing.
Modes of travel: Horse, foot, and canoe.
Maps: Glenwood Ranger District map; Snowden-VA 1:24,000 topo map.

OVERVIEW: Established in 1975, James River Face could be called the grand-daddy of the Virginia wilderness system. The first of sixteen areas in the commonwealth to be protected under the Wilderness Act, James River Face is located on the northern end of Thunder Ridge, a long ridge of the Blue Ridge Mountains. The James River borders the north end of the wilderness, Forest Road 95 borders the southern end, and the Blue Ridge Parkway forms the eastern border. This primitive area includes the entire western slope of the Blue Ridge and the upper portions of the eastern side. The region bordering the James River is extremely steep, and there is very little safe access to the river itself. The southern end of the wilderness lies on the upper reaches of Thunder Ridge.

James River Face could best be characterized as a relatively dry region. Several small springs originate from remote regions within the wilderness boundaries, but there are no major creeks within the James River Face Wilderness. Therefore, it is best to pack water when hiking through the area.

The oak-hickory forest dominates the wilderness. There are, however, scattered pockets of white pine, hemlock, chestnut oak, and Virginia pine. Much of the Virginia pine in the James River Face has been affected by the Southern pine bark beetle and is dead or dying. The woolly adelgid has found a foothold within the wilderness boundary and is affecting hemlock populations.

There are several features of special interest within the wilderness. Devils Marble Yard is notable for its numerous large boulders. This intriguing site encompasses several acres along Belfast Trail and showcases boulders that are often

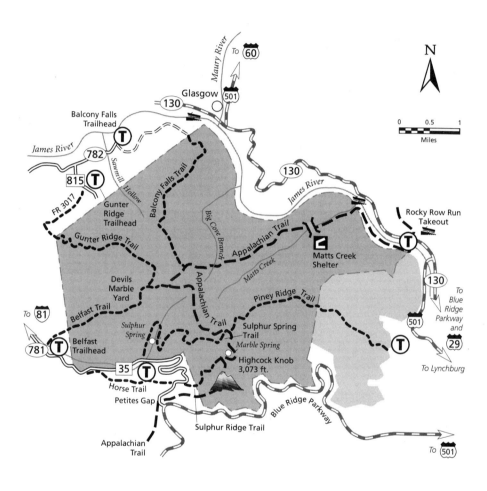

larger than a school bus. There is also a small waterfall cascading over a rock wall on the trails leading past the Marble Yard. Another area of interest is Marble Spring, a small spring located just off of the Appalachian Trail near Highcock Knob. At 3,073 feet, Highcock Knob is the highest point in the James River Face. The summit is easy to reach via the Appalachian Trail's southern trailhead, and is well worth the trip for its tremendous vista to the east.

RECREATIONAL USES: The trail system throughout the wilderness is extensive. The wilderness has approximately 27 miles of trails that are generally well maintained. The Sulphur Ridge Trail is the only trail in the wilderness area that is not highly maintained. It exits the James River Face Wilderness, crosses FR 35, and enters the Thunder Ridge Wilderness. Although not officially maintained, it is nevertheless in excellent condition. Except for the southern end of the Appalachian Trail, the trails begin at the base of the mountains and climb to ridge crests. This characteristic might be a deterrent to some, but the hiking is excellent.

Horseback riding is a favorite activity within the boundaries of this wilderness area. The Piney Ridge Trail is a popular destination for riders of all skills, as are the Gunter Ridge Trail and the Sulphur Spring Trail.

Day Hike

Belfast Trail/Sulphur Spring Trail Loop

Distance: 9.3 miles.
Difficulty: Moderate to strenuous.
Topo map: Snowden-VA.

HOW TO GET THERE: *From Lexington,* take Interstate 81 south to exit 180. Take US 11 south 3.5 miles to Virginia Highway 130. Turn left on VA 130 and proceed 3.2 miles to County Road 759. Turn right on CR 759, travel 3.2 miles, and turn left on CR 781. Travel 1.3 miles to the parking area on the left.

From Lynchburg, take US 29 north to VA 130; turn left (west) on VA 130. Proceed 29 miles, turning left toward Glasgow, and turn left on CR 759. Drive 3.2 miles to a left turn on CR 781 and continue 1.3 miles to the parking area on the left.

The Belfast Trail begins by crossing a bridge over the East Fork. The distance to the Devils Marble Yard is 1 mile, the Gunter Ridge Trail is 2 miles, and the Appalachian Trail is 3 miles. The trail maintains an easy grade for the first 0.5 mile, passing the foundations of several old structures. After crossing two small creeks, the grade becomes moderate. The Belfast Trail is lined with ferns and large cove hardwoods.

The path becomes very steep. The Devils Marble Yard can be seen on the left, and there is a small waterfall on the right. Just beyond the waterfall, a short trail leads to the Marble Yard at 1 mile. This region of large boulders extends down the entire slope of the mountain, covering several acres. From the boulder field there is an excellent view of the Thunder Ridge Wilderness and the upper end of Arnolds Valley.

Beyond the Devils Marble Yard, the Belfast Trail continues to climb and intersects with the Gunter Ridge Trail. At this intersection, continue straight another 0.5 mile to the junction with the AT, where there is a small campsite surrounded by several large oaks. At the trail junction, turn right on the AT and head south.

The AT begins to descend at a leisurely pace. The trail is well maintained and marked with white blazes. There are beautiful views to the south, mostly of Thunder Ridge. Pine and chestnut oak dominate this dry region. Many of the pines are dead, victims of the Southern pine bark beetle. The trail joins an old road before reaching a junction with several other trails, about 1.8 miles from the Belfast Trail.

Turn right on the Sulphur Spring Trail and begin a gradual 2.7-mile descent along an old road to FR 35. About 0.9 mile from the junction, a rock outcrop on the left affords a panoramic view to the south and west. The trail continues to descend to Sulphur Spring, where it makes a left bend. Continue 0.5 mile to FR 35, turn right, and walk 1.8 miles back to the parking area.

View of Devils Marble Yard along the Belfast Trail.

Day Hike

Balcony Falls/Gunter Ridge Trail Loop

Distance: 13.1 miles.
Difficulty: Moderate to strenuous.
Topo map: Snowden-VA.

HOW TO GET THERE: *From Lexington,* take Interstate 81 south to exit 180. Take US 11 south 3.5 miles to Virginia Highway 130. Turn left on VA 130 and proceed 3.2 miles to County Road 759. Turn right on CR 759, travel 0.8 mile, and turn left on CR 782. Continue 1.7 miles to the parking area.

From Lynchburg, take US 29 north to VA 130; turn left (west) on VA 130. Proceed 29 miles, turning left toward Glasgow, and turn left on CR 759. Drive 0.8 mile, turn left on CR 782, and continue 1.7 miles to the parking area.

This loop begins by passing through a small meadow to a Forest Service information center. The first mile is a gradual descent—enjoy this while it lasts. At the end of the descent, the Balcony Falls Trail begins a difficult climb to the ridge crest. There are a total of twenty-two switchbacks during this climb. Three miles into the hike, the crest is reached, and there is a beautiful view of the valley below.

The next section of the trail follows the ridge to the summit. The views from this trail are spectacular and instill a feeling of being on top of the world. Once on the ridge, the Balcony Falls Trail begins to meander along at an easy grade. At about 5 miles a sign reads SAWMILL HOLLOW; not far beyond is the junction with the Appalachian Trail.

Follow the AT south along the ridge. After about 0.5 mile, the AT intersects with the Belfast Trail. At this intersection there is a nice spot to camp beneath an imposing stand of oak trees. Turn right on the Belfast Trail and continue another 0.5 mile to the junction with the Gunter Ridge Trail; turn right.

The Gunter Ridge Trail begins with a moderate descent down the mountain. After a short distance, the grade becomes steeper, passing through about fifteen switchbacks. After crossing a small creek, the grade becomes much easier. About 4 miles from the trail junction, the Gunter Ridge Trail intersects with a gravel road (FR 3017). Turn right and follow the road about 1.25 miles to a gate and a large parking area. Continue past the parking area and follow CR 815 for about 0.75 mile until it intersects with CR 782. Turn right on CR 782 and walk 1.1 miles to the trailhead parking area for the Balcony Falls Trail.

Day Hike

Appalachian Trail

Distance: 10.2 miles one way.
Difficulty: Moderate.
Topo map: Snowden-VA.

HOW TO GET THERE: *Lower parking area—From Lexington,* take Interstate 81 south to exit 180. Turn south on US 11 and proceed 4.4 miles to the intersection of US 11 and Virginia Highway 130. Turn left on VA 130 and travel 6.4 miles to the intersection of VA 130 and US 501. Turn right on US 501/VA 130 and drive 6.1 miles to the AT parking lot on the right.

From Lynchburg, take US 29 north to VA 130; turn left (west) on VA 130. Proceed 20.2 miles to the AT parking lot on the left.

Upper parking area—Take the Blue Ridge Parkway to milepost 71 at Petites Gap. Turn west on Forest Road 35 and proceed 0.1 mile to the parking area on the right.

From the lower parking area on VA 130, the trail crosses the James River via the James River Foot Bridge. On the opposite bank is a right switchback, and the AT begins to parallel the James River upstream for approximately 1 mile. The trail is a series of very easy ups and downs. In several places, short pawpaw trees line the trail. There is no camping allowed along the first mile of the trail.

At 1 mile the trail bends left and enters the Matts Creek watershed. With Matts Creek on the right, the trail climbs gradually upstream. The creek tumbles over many small rapids on its quick descent to the James River. Just before reaching the shelter, a blue blazed trail exits to the left. This is the old AT, which leads back to US 501 and a trailhead on the south side of the James River just past the Snowden Bridge.

Matts Creek Shelter is a pleasant place to rest and obtain water. Just past the shelter, cross the stream via a man-made bridge, then begin a long, moderate uphill grade. The crest of the finger ridge is reached at about the 3.5-mile mark. To the right there are several rocks and an overlook from which the town of Glasgow and House Mountain are visible. The trail contours the mountain for a short distance and then continues its uphill course. After a stream crossing, the trail moves rapidly up the mountain. There are several switchbacks during this climb. Near the end of the climb, the AT meets the Balcony Falls Trail, which exits to the right at the 5.5-mile mark.

After another 0.5 mile of contouring, the AT reaches the intersection with the Belfast Trail. There is a small campsite at this junction. The Belfast Trail exits to the right; the AT goes to the left and starts downhill. There are some beautiful views to the south. Pine and chestnut oak dominate this dry region. The next trail junction, at 7.7 miles, is the intersection of the AT, the Piney Ridge Trail, and the Sulphur Spring Trail. The distance to Petites Gap is 2.75 miles.

Continue on the AT as it starts an easy 0.5-mile descent to Marble Spring, which sits in a saddle between Piney Ridge and Highcock Knob. Marble Spring is to the right of the trail, downhill about 300 feet. This area is a good place to spend the night. The AT crosses the saddle and begins climbing Highcock Knob. About 0.3 mile beyond the Marble Spring area, the Sulphur Ridge Trail exits to the right, leading to the Thunder Ridge Wilderness.

Past the junction, there is a short flat section before the steep, difficult climb up to the summit of the knob. At 3,073 feet, the summit of Highcock Knob is the highest point in the James River Face Wilderness. The summit is flat and there is a view of the piedmont region of Virginia. On the opposite side of the summit, the trail begins to descend to FR 35. Initially, this descent is steep, but the grade becomes easy when the AT enters the Petites Gap region. There is a Forest Service information center at the parking area.

Canoe Trip

James River from Glasgow to Snowden

Distance: 4 to 5 miles.
Difficulty: Some Class III and IV rapids.
Topo map: Snowden-VA.

HOW TO GET THERE: In Glasgow, take the dirt road that leads to the put-in area on the Maury River. This road, located near the railroad tracks and the Maury River Bridge, turns toward the river.

This section of the James River breaks through the Blue Ridge Mountains into the piedmont of Virginia. The ridges are steep and lined with cliffs. This run is not for the novice canoeist or kayaker, especially when the water is running high. The normal level for the river is approximately 6 inches. The put-in at Locher Landing is located near the train trestle crossing the Maury River. The first difficult spot is the confluence of the James River and the Maury River. Many large boulders dot the river, some of which are suitable for eddy play.

Past the confluence, the river becomes wider. The steep cliffs of the James River Face are on the right. Shortly after entering the James, the first obstacle is a small set of rapids that used to be a part of the old Balcony Falls dam, which was removed years ago. After this set of rapids, the James enters the Balcony Falls. The rapids here begin with some small ledges for practice.

The James River Face and the James River below.

Past these first ledges, there is a series of several more to contend with. Depending on the route selected, the runs can be easy or require a high level of maneuvering skills. It is always best to scout the rapids before attempting to run them. The James then becomes more forgiving. There are a few Class II ledges and rock gardens before reaching the impoundment behind the Snowden dam. Upon exiting the Balcony Falls region, a flat sandy area on the right side of the river is a great place to stop and have lunch. There are several takeouts along the left side of the river. The last of these, Rocky Row Run, enters the James from the left just before the dam.

East Coast

Virginia Coast Reserve

Location: 20 miles north of Virginia Beach, Virginia.
Size: 45,000-acre coast reserve.
Administration: Jointly administered by the Nature Conservancy, the Virginia Department of Game and Inland Fisheries, and the U.S. Fish and Wildlife Service.
Management status: Nature preserve.
Ecosystems: Tidal marshlands and pine hummocks.
Elevation range: ⁻5 to 20 feet.
System trails: None.
Maximum core-to-perimeter distance: 15 miles.
Activities: Canoeing, kayaking, swimming, bird-watching, and fishing. Hunting is allowed on Mockhorn Island.
Modes of travel: Boat.
Maps: GMCO map of Virginia Barrier Islands (not 1:24,000); Accomac-VA, Bloxom-VA, Cheriton-VA, Cobb Island-VA, Metompkin Inlet-VA, Nassawadox-VA, Quinby Inlet-VA, Townsend-VA, Ship Shoal Inlet-VA, Wachapreague-VA, and Wallops Island-VA 1:24,000 topo maps.

OVERVIEW: The barrier islands of Virginia are a unique geological feature on the East Coast. Many of the islands exist only when the tide is low. The conservation effort for these islands was started in the mid-1950s by the Nature Conservancy. Since those humble beginnings, almost 45,000 acres of barrier islands and tidal marshes have been placed under permanent protection. Protected regions include forests on pine hummocks, salt marshes of cordgrass, and sandy beaches. These islands also serve to protect the mainland from the pounding of ocean waves, which have been slowly pushing the islands toward the mainland for thousands of years. Therefore, the shape of the barrier islands is constantly changing.

Many of the islands are dry only during low tides. When the tide is high, these same islands become vast, shallow salt marshes covered with marsh grasses. A good example of this is Mockhorn Island, which is owned by the state of Virginia and managed by the Department of Game and Inland Fisheries. When the tide is low, the island is almost totally above the water, but as the tide rises the land slowly submerges, and only the pine hummocks remain above sea level. This is true for much of the marshlands along the eastern shore.

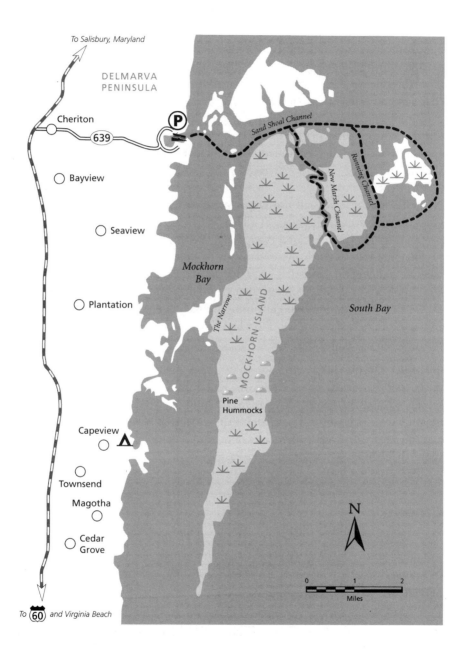

To Salisbury, Maryland

DELMARVA
PENINSULA

Cheriton

639

Bayview

Seaview

Plantation

Capeview

Townsend

Magotha

Cedar
Grove

To 60 and Virginia Beach

Sand Shoal Channel

Running Channel

New Marsh Channel

Mockhorn
Bay

The Narrows

MOCKHORN ISLAND

South Bay

Pine
Hummocks

N

0   1   2
Miles

These tidal marshlands and barrier islands teem with life. The Nature Conservancy estimates that there are as many as 250 species of raptors, songbirds, and waterfowl that take up residence in the reserve throughout the year. The coast reserve serves as the nesting grounds for tens of thousands of birds during the breeding season from April to October. It is best to stay away from the marshes during these times to avoid disturbing the birds, many of which nest in the marshes or on the ground. When paddling through the area, stay in the channels and out of the marshes.

Camping is permitted only on the pine hummocks of Mockhorn Island. On the Wreck Island Natural Area Preserve, hunting, fishing, camping, fires, and unleashed pets are prohibited. Hunting, overnight camping, fires, and pets are also prohibited on land managed by the Nature Conservancy. Parts of these islands may be closed at any time. To find out more about the Wreck Island Natural Area Preserve, call the Department of Conservation and Recreation, Division of Natural Heritage, at (804) 786–7951. To find out about lands managed by the Nature Conservancy, call (800) 628–6860.

The only way to reach these islands is by boat. For safety purposes, carry a compass and a good chart that gives depths and channel markings. If traveling in a canoe or sea kayak, be aware that paddling against the tide and the wind can be extremely difficult and at times impossible. Also, some of the channels and bays can become very choppy when the wind is up. *Note:* Be aware of the weather, the tides, and the time.

RECREATIONAL USES: Bird-watching is the primary recreational activity in the barrier islands. As noted above, the region is home to at least 250 different species of birds. If fishing is your sport, many different types of fish can be caught along the eastern shore. Each fish has its own size limit and creel limit. Consult with the Department of Game and Inland Fisheries to learn more about the fishing regulations for the eastern shore.

Canoe trip

New Marsh Channel

Distance: 14.5 miles.
Difficulty: Moderate to strenuous, depending on tides and wind direction.
Topo maps: Cheriton-VA and Cobb Island-VA.

HOW TO GET THERE: From Virginia Beach, cross the Chesapeake Bay Bridge–Tunnel to Cape Charles on the Delmarva Peninsula. The fee for the bridge is $10. From the north, drive south on US 13 from Salisbury, Maryland. About 12 miles from the southern tip of the Delmarva Peninsula, take Alternate US 13 into the town of Cheriton. Turn east on Sunnyside Road (County Road 639) and go 2.4 miles to Crumb Hill Road. A sign for a public boat landing marks the turn. Drive 0.7 mile to the boat landing on the Oyster Slip.

Begin this trip at the landing in Oyster Community. Paddle down the Oyster Slip to the Ramshorn Channel, turn to the right, and paddle a short distance to the Sand Shoal Channel. Cross the channel to the G "233" channel marker near the northern end of Mockhorn Island. Paddle about 1.3 miles east to a small channel that enters the island. There are no channel markers after entering the island. The channel travels generally south in a series of horseshoe bends. After about 3.5 miles, New Marsh Channel breaks out into South Bay.

If seas are calm, turn east and hug the shoreline of Mockhorn Island. Paddle about 1.4 miles and enter Running Channel. Follow Running Channel north back to Sand Shoal Channel. The channel marker at the end of the Running Channel is G "9." The trip can be made slightly longer by paddling east past Running Channel and around the Man and Boy Marsh, through a small channel that enters the Sand Shoal Channel at G "227."

The only place to spend the night throughout the entire region is on Mockhorn Island. The only dry land on the island is located in the central portion near The Narrows. The rest of the island is submerged during high tides.

North River Landing Nature Preserve 29

Location: Virginia Beach, Virginia.
Size: 10,000 acres.
Administration: The Nature Conservancy.
Management status: 10,000-acre nonfederal wilderness nature preserve.
Ecosystems: Tidal marsh, swamp forestlands, wetlands, and black-water creeks.
Elevation range: 0 to 5 feet.
System trails: No maintained trails.
Maximum core-to-perimeter distance: 0.8 mile.
Activities: Canoeing, fishing, and bird-watching.
Modes of travel: Canoe.
Maps: Pleasant Ridge-VA and Creeds-VA and NC 1:24,000 topo maps.

OVERVIEW: The North River Landing Nature Preserve protects an interesting land formation known as a *pocosin*. A pocosin is swampy land, and is one of the fastest-disappearing landforms in the United States. Long considered to be an annoyance, these lands were channeled to drain the water in an attempt to make them suitable for agricultural use. However, times have changed, and some of these lands are now being protected to preserve the wildlife habitat they offer.

The North River Landing Nature Preserve seeks to do just that. Although not protected under the Wilderness Act, the lands of the preserve have been bought by the Nature Conservancy and placed under protection. This preserve is made up of wetlands, forested swamps, freshwater tidal marshes, and open water. One unique feature of the preserve is that the tides, if they can be called that, are governed primarily by the winds. This means that water levels fluctuate when the wind changes direction.

The preserve protects the habitat of several rare species of plants, including sawgrass, rose mallow, and red milkweed cypress. According to the Virginia Department of Conservation, twenty-seven rare species of plants are protected here. The nature preserve also provides breeding habitat for many bird species and wintering grounds for many types of waterfowl. Water-loving mammals are also common, but don't expect to see many, as most are nocturnal. Several different types of reptiles and amphibians can be seen while paddling the waters of the many small creeks along the North Landing River. Mud turtles and

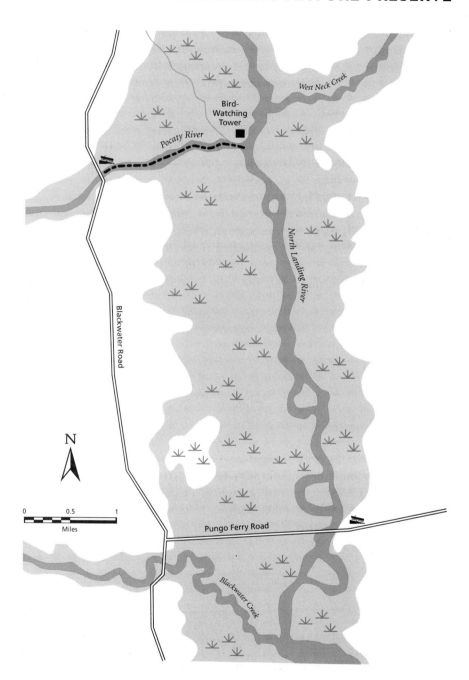

West Neck Creek

Bird-
Watching
Tower

Pocaty River

North Landing River

Blackwater Road

N

0   0.5   1
Miles

Pungo Ferry Road

Blackwater Creek

snapping turtles are the most common. Several species of snakes live here, including the venomous water moccasin.

At times these sensitive areas are closed to the public to protect the fragile environment of the wetlands. For information on the North River Landing Preserve, contact the Department of Conservation and Recreation at (757) 481–2131 or the Nature Conservancy at (800) 628–6860.

RECREATIONAL USES: Recreational use in the nature preserve is confined to water travel. Canoeing along the Pocaty River and the Blackwater Creek offers the visitor a short trip into a land time forgot. Both creeks are flat and slow moving, and the water is so dark that it is impossible to see the bottom except in the very shallow areas.

The North River Landing Nature Preserve is a bird-watcher's paradise. The region is on the flyway for neotropical birds migrating to warmer climates. Some of these birds spend the winter months in and around the tidal marshes of the preserve. Fall and spring are the best times to view migrating birds. Another popular activity is wildflower identification. The unique ecosystem allows viewing of plants that would normally be seen much farther south.

Canoe trip

Pocaty River

Distance: 3 miles round-trip.
Difficulty: Easy.
Topo map: Pleasant Ridge-VA.

HOW TO GET THERE: On Interstate 64 at Virginia Beach, take exit 290-B. Drive 4.1 miles south on Battlefield Boulevard and take a left on Mount Pleasant Road. Drive 7.9 miles east to Fentress Road and turn right on Blackwater Road. Continue 0.1 mile and take a left on Blackwater Road. Go 2.6 miles to a bridge and the Pocaty River. Park on the left side of the road.

Put your canoe in the Pocaty River at the bridge and begin paddling downstream. Initially, the river is narrow, and fallen trees lie partially across it. None of the downfall is difficult to paddle around. The river passes through forested swamps, and several smaller streams branch off to the right and the left. Many birds, such as great blue herons, kingfishers, and red-winged blackbirds, can be seen along the river. After passing several small islands, watch for a major creek that joins the Pocaty from the left. This creek can be paddled upstream for about 0.5 mile. While paddling this small branch, be on the lookout for turtles and snakes.

The flat, calm Pocaty River.

Back at the confluence, continue east on the Pocaty River. The river begins to widen, the forest backs away, and marsh grasses invade the shoreline. Through this stretch, travel close to the bank for the best views of the abundant birds and wildlife. Just before the Pocaty meets the North Landing River, a tower and landing dock are on the left side of the river. Stop here for a wonderful view of the marsh grasses and bird life that exist along the river. If you want a longer trip, turn south on the North Landing River and paddle approximately 4.4 miles to the Pungo Road Bridge. There is a takeout on the left side of the river.

Although the land on both sides of the Pocaty is a nature preserve, the rivers are considered navigable waters. Therefore, motorboats do travel up the Pocaty about 1 mile from the North Landing River. Watch for wakes that could tip your canoe. The land to the west of the North Landing River is also a part of the preserve, but the North Landing River is part of the Intercoastal Waterway. Large boats travel this waterway frequently. Please exercise caution while traveling this river.

Shenandoah National Park

Shenandoah National Park   **30**

Location: 75 miles west of Washington, D.C., just south of the Front Royal, Virginia, city limits.
Size: 196,466 acres of National Park land; 79,579 acres in ten designated wilderness units.
Administration: National Park Service.
Management status: National Park.
Ecosystems: Eastern deciduous forest.
Elevation range: 700 to 4,014 feet.
System trails: More than 500 miles.
Maximum core-to-perimeter distance: 3 miles.
Activities: Hiking, backpacking, camping, fishing, and horseback riding.
Modes of travel: Foot and horse.
Maps: Shenandoah National Park maps: Northern, Central, and Southern (1:62,500 scale); Crimora-VA, Grottoes-VA, McGaheysville-VA, and Old Rag Mountain-VA 1:24,000 topo maps.

OVERVIEW: Located within miles of some of the most populated areas in the East, Shenandoah National Park is a stronghold of wildness. The park, long and thin, stretches from Front Royal south to Waynesboro along the Blue Ridge escarpment. Skyline Drive bisects the park. Ten wilderness areas within the park flank Skyline Drive, totaling more than 79,000 acres. These areas cover peaks, valleys, waterfalls, and pastures on mountains that are more than 250 million years old. Wind and rain have caused these mountains to crumble, leaving granite outcrops, boulder-strewn peaks, and ribbons of rocks cascading down mountainsides. The rocks are the exception and not the norm, though. Shenandoah National Park is most well known for its beautiful views, rolling mountains, and diverse wildlife.

The park was established in December 1935. President Herbert Hoover touted the park as a way for drivers to see the wonderful views from the tops of the Blue Ridge Mountains. Shenandoah National Park is effectively separated into thirds by roads and entrance stations along the way. The north section runs from Front Royal to Thornton Gap, where US 211 crosses Skyline Drive. The middle section is from Thornton Gap to Swift Run Gap and US 33. The southern section follows the park down to Interstate 64 and US 250. There are park entrances at both ends of the park, as well as at the intersections of US 211 and US 33. Wilderness areas are fairly evenly distributed, with three in the southern section, four in the middle, and three more in the north.

30A SHENANDOAH NATIONAL PARK (OVERVIEW)

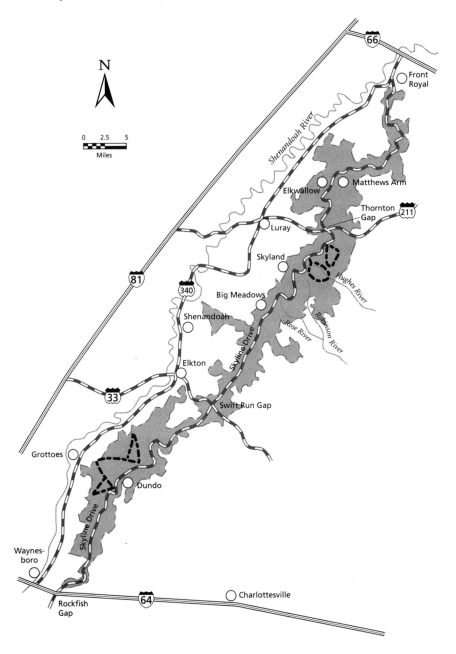

Wildlife is abundant in the park; the animals enjoy the protection afforded by the park boundaries. Shenandoah is home to the largest black bear population in the commonwealth. Hikers have a good chance of seeing a bear on park trails. Backpackers should hang their food or store it in bear-resistant containers. Deer occupy the park in large numbers. Some have even become quite accustomed to the passing of cars on Skyline Drive. Other residents include wild turkeys, foxes, squirrels, and bobcats. Bird-watchers take special note of the southern tip of the park around Rockfish Gap. Here the gap creates a natural flyway for hawks on their annual migration.

With all of its wild beauty, the park does have development and various facilities. After all, the park is split down the middle by a road. The following is a list of facilities along Skyline Drive:

Campgrounds	(mile)	Lodges	(mile)
Matthews Arm	(22.2)	Skyland Lodge	(41.7)
Big Meadows	(51)	Big Meadows	(51)
Lewis Mountain	(57.6)	Lewis Mountain	(57.6)
Loft Mountain	(79.5)		
Dundo Group Campground	(83.7)		

Restaurants	(mile)	Stores	(mile)
Elkwallow Wayside	(24.1)	Elkwallow	(24.1)
Panorama Restaurant	(31.5)	Big Meadows	(51)
Skyland Lodge	(41.7)	Lewis Mountain	(57.6)
Big Meadows	(51)	Loft Mountain	(79.5)
Loft Mountain	(79.5)		

Campgrounds are first-come first-served, except Dundo Group Campground and Big Meadows (May through late November only), which are by reservation. Also, sections of the park are closed during winter months. Check with park headquarters prior to your visit.

RECREATIONAL USES: Covering nearly 200,000 acres of the beautiful Blue Ridge Mountains of Virginia, Shenandoah National Park has wonderful opportunities for hikers, backpackers, campers, horseback riders, and anglers. Fall foliage brings the highest concentration of tourists. Most view the colors from Skyline Drive, but a number hike the trails and use the backcountry. If solitude is your goal, October is not the time to visit Shenandoah. All times of the year are beautiful in this park, though. The turning of the seasons is marked by changes in the forest, and the trail is a wonderful place to view these variations.

Most Shenandoah streams are a mix of boulders and pools. The cold, aerated water provides the perfect habitat for brook trout.

There are more than 500 miles of trails in Shenandoah National Park. Trails are blazed as follows: White is the Appalachian Trail, blue designates hiking trails, and yellow is for horse trails. On a horse trail, the horse has the right-of-way. There are long and short rides on wilderness trails and park fire roads. For recommendations, contact park headquarters. Backcountry camping is allowed throughout most of the park, but a permit is required. Permits are free and can be obtained at entrance stations, visitor centers, park headquarters, or by mail. Contact Shenandoah National Park, 3655 US 211E, Luray, VA 22835-9036, (540) 999–3500.

Day hikers are encouraged to sign in at one of the trail registers. Fires are permitted only at trail shelters. For those who like to hike with man's best friend, dogs are permitted on most trails, but a 6-foot leash is required. Dogs are prohibited on some trails, so check at the entrance station for information on the trails you plan to hike.

Fishing in the park requires patience and persistence. Thirty streams in the park are open for fishing. Anglers must release any fish they catch, and single-hook artificial lures are required by law. Fishing season goes year-round, but a valid Virginia fishing license is needed. Although some streams are stocked with rainbow and brown trout outside the park boundary, native brook trout is the dominant species within the park. Two popular streams are the Rose and the Robinson Rivers on the east side of Skyline Drive. Several west-side streams also provide good fishing. Check with park headquarters for the latest information.

Given that Skyline Drive is 105 miles long, there are many places to access the park. The main entrance at Front Royal is along US 340 on the south side of town. The central section can be accessed via US 211 at Thornton Gap. From Luray, the entrance to the central section of the park is 9 miles east. US 33 crosses Skyline Drive at Swift Run Gap just east of Elkton. The southern entrance is located just off Interstate 64 at Rockfish Gap, near Waynesboro. Along the perimeter of the park, access points are abundant. Care should be taken, though, to avoid crossing private property. Also, if you are accessing the park along the perimeter and planning to stay overnight in the backcountry, make sure you have the proper permit.

Day Hike

Hazel Mountain/Hannah Run Loop

Distance: 10.4 miles.
Difficulty: Moderate.
Topo map: Old Rag Mountain-VA.

30B SHENANDOAH NATIONAL PARK (NORTHERN SECTION)

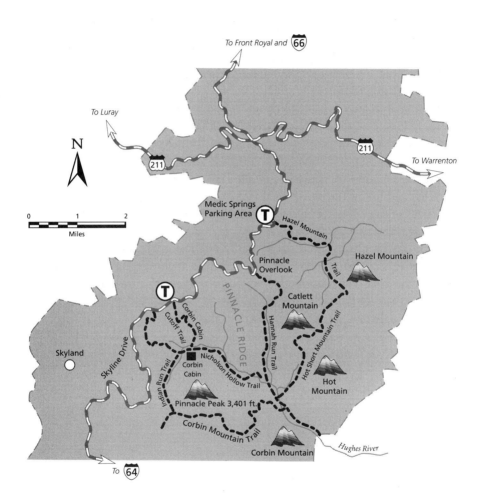

HOW TO GET THERE: From the junction with US 211, go south on Skyline Drive to the Medic Springs parking area on the east side of the road.

This is a moderately difficult loop hike in a well-used portion of the park. The trail steadily loses altitude to the intersection with Nicholson Hollow Trail, then climbs its way back up the ridge along Hannah Run Trail. There are many interconnecting trails in this area, so be careful to stay on the correct path. The grade is predominantly easy, but expect steep, strenuous sections toward the lower end of Hot Short Mountain Trail and the upper end of Hannah Run Trail. These trails follow streams for much of their length, so water is readily available for filtering.

The hike follows Hazel Mountain Trail 4.2 miles to Hot Short Mountain Trail. Hiking along the yellow-blazed Hazel Mountain Trail is easy to moderate through stands of pine, oak, and hickory. Other trails cross the route, but concrete pylons at each junction point directions.

At the junction of Hazel Mountain Trail and Hot Short Mountain Trail, turn left and follow the blue-blazed Hot Short Mountain Trail, which contours gradually at first, then turns steep and rocky. At one point the trail skirts an interesting stand of locust trees.

The trail eventually levels out and joins Nicholson Hollow Trail. Turn right and follow Nicholson Hollow Trail for 0.3 mile, then turn right onto Hannah Run Trail. This trail follows Hannah Run, a tributary of the Hughes River, along the base of Pinnacle Ridge. The hiking is steady and the stream is gorgeous. Large hemlock and cove hardwoods thrive here. The stream shrinks into nothingness as the ridge becomes steeper. Soon the trail climbs madly up the ridge in three sections. The first leads to Catlett Mountain Trail; the second yields at a small knob and saddle between Catlett Mountain and The Pinnacle. The final climb is to Skyline Drive, and hikers are rewarded with views from Pinnacle Overlook. Hike north 1.5 miles along Skyline Drive to return to the Medic Springs parking area and the beginning of the hike.

Day Hike

Corbin Cabin Loop

Distance: 11 miles.
Difficulty: Moderate.
Topo map: Old Rag Mountain-VA.

HOW TO GET THERE: From US 211, drive south on Skyline Drive to a parking lot and trailhead between mileposts 37 and 38.

Begin at the Corbin Cabin Cutoff Trail. The concrete trailhead marker puts the distance to the cabin at 1.4 miles. The blue-blazed trail descends rapidly through a corridor of mountain laurel. After a right switchback, the descent becomes more gradual, then the trail parallels a small creek, crossing it once, to Corbin Cabin. An old rock wall marks the entrance to the cabin area. Corbin Cabin is an old log structure maintained by the National Park Service. It is available for use, but reservations are required.

At the cabin, the trail joins Nicholson Hollow Trail. Turn right on Nicholson Hollow Trail and go 0.2 mile to another trail junction under a stand of tall red oak and hickory. Bear left at this junction on Indian Run Trail, which climbs gradually and then very steeply to a lush green saddle. Ferns, fringed bleeding heart, and striped maple line the trail in the saddle. After crossing through this small saddle, the trail descends gradually, reaching the Corbin Mountain Trail after 1.6 miles.

Turn left on the Corbin Mountain Trail, which descends gradually through a forest of oak and hickory. Many of the oaks have died as a result of a gypsy moth infestation. After about 1.3 miles, the trail makes a steep descent to a small creek, then contours along the side of the ridge and makes another steep drop to the Hughes River. Small hemlocks form the overstory near the river. Cross the river, which can be difficult when the water is high, and join Nicholson Hollow Trail about 3.8 miles from the beginning of the Corbin Mountain Trail.

Turn left on Nicholson Hollow Trail and follow the Hughes River upstream. The trail is wide and easy to follow. Corbin Cabin is 2.8 miles from this junction. The Hot Short Mountain Trail exits to the right; after a short distance the Hannah Run Trail also goes right. In this vicinity, a stone wall parallels the trail. Before reaching Corbin Cabin, there is one more creek crossing, which can also be difficult during high water. Large boulders make this area very scenic. Once back at Corbin Cabin, turn right on the Corbin Cabin Cutoff Trail to return to the parking lot and trailhead.

Day Hike or Backpack

Rockytop/Big Run Portal Loop

Distance: 18.5 miles.
Difficulty: Strenuous.
Topo maps: McGaheysville-VA and Grottoes-VA.

HOW TO GET THERE: From Interstate 81, about halfway between Staunton and Harrisonburg, take exit 235. At the stop sign turn east onto County Road 256 and drive 6.6 miles to the town of Grottoes. Turn left at the stop sign, drive 0.1 mile, and turn right on County Road 663. At the caution light, go straight across the intersection and continue east on CR 663. Drive 2.6 miles

to gravel Madison Run Road. Continue straight another 0.1 mile and park on the left where a private drive joins the road. A gate on Madison Run Road marks the park boundary.

This hike incorporates several trails to create a wonderfully picturesque loop on the western slopes of the park. There are views into the park to the east, out to the Shenandoah Valley to the west, and of Massanutten Mountain to the north. After traveling across the ridge top, the trail makes equal time along the shady banks of Big Run. Although completely delightful and highly recommended, this hike is long and difficult. Climbs up and down Austin Mountain are steep and littered with rocks. Strong legs are needed to hike this trail. For backpackers, the best campsites are near the northern end of Big Run Portal Trail.

Before leaving your car, take a moment to make sure you have an adequate water supply. Once you start up Austin Mountain, there are no water sources until Big Run, 8.5 miles away. From the parking lot, hike about 0.5 mile east along Madison Run Road. Turn left on Austin Mountain Trail and start up the ridge.

Austin Mountain Trail climbs 3.2 miles to the ridge top of Austin Mountain. The trail is steep, rugged, and littered with rocks. At times rocks *are* the trail. Although tough, the hike is wonderfully rewarding. The rocky sections provide breaks in the canopy, which afford views of the ridges to the south. There are many excellent views of Furnace Mountain and Luck Hollow. The views and exposure also allow you to get a good sense of the altitude you're gaining and encourage you to continue the climb.

The trail eventually levels off, but then makes a final climb to the ridge crest and a junction with Rockytop Trail. Go left and follow Rockytop Trail north 5.3 miles to the lower end of Big Run Portal Trail. Rockytop Trail is a picturesque hike along the crest of the ridge. There are many wonderful views of the park to the east and the Shenandoah Valley to the west. A highlight of this section is Rockytop, a boulder-covered peak with views of Lewis Peak and the Shenandoah Valley to the west, and of Massanutten Mountain to the north. The descent off Rockytop is long and gradual. There are a couple of switchbacks as the junction with Big Run Portal Trail nears, but this hike down is much gentler than the hike up. There is no water source along Rockytop Trail.

Turn right on the yellow-blazed Big Run Portal Trail (a left here leads to private property), which follows Big Run 4.3 miles to join Big Run Loop Trail. There are excellent campsites near large pools of water toward the lower end of the trail. The hike up Big Run is easy to moderate, passing through stands of laurel, tulip poplar, white pine, and mature oak-hickory forests. There are several stream crossings, and you will pass Brown Mountain, Rocky Mountain Run, and Patterson Ridge Trails along the way. The climb grows steeper farther up the run, and the forest changes to mature cove hardwoods, hemlock, and white pine. The middle canopy is nonexistent and the understory consists of a single species—a certain ground-hugging ivy with leaves of three.

Soon the trail meets Big Run Loop Trail. One of the first things you'll notice about the Big Run Loop is that it is a popular hike. Beginning at the Big Run Overlook on Skyline Drive, the trail is a short loop linking Rockytop Trail and the Appalachian Trail. Chances are you won't see anyone on your hike until you reach this point. At the intersection, turn right and follow Big Run Loop toward Rockytop Trail, 1.3 miles away. This section of the hike is characterized by long moderate climbs with few turns. The trail makes a right switchback, moves away from the stream drainage, and continues on a moderate ascent. As altitude is gained, trees become smaller. A stand of dead trees, which continues down the ridge, is reached, and soon the trail arrives at the ridge crest and the junction with Rockytop Trail.

From the junction, turn right and follow Rockytop 0.4 mile to Austin Mountain Trail. Retrace your tracks 3.2 miles down the ridge to Madison Run Road. Be careful on the way down Austin Mountain: The rocky trail and steep angle add extra stress to knees, and by this point legs are weary. Enjoy the afternoon views of Furnace Mountain. Back on Madison Run Road, turn right and head back to your car.

Day Hike or Overnight

Furnace Mountain Summit Day Hike or Black Hut Springs Loop

Distance: 5.6 miles or 15.6 miles.
Difficulty: Moderate.
Topo maps: Crimora-VA and Grottoes-VA.

HOW TO GET THERE: Follow the preceding directions to the trailhead for the Rockytop/Big Run Portal Loop hike.

From the parking area, walk up the gravel road past the gate to the Furnace Mountain Trailhead on the right. A concrete post with a metal band near the top marks the trailhead. The Furnace Mountain Trail is well marked with blue blazes and is usually clear of brush and debris. The trail crosses Madison Run, which can be difficult when the water is high, then climbs to a long ridge and continues a steady ascent for 2.3 miles. Initially, the forest is composed of small oak and hickory. As you cross to the drier western side of the ridge, the oak and hickory give way to small Virginia pine and pitch pine. Many of the pines are dead, victims of the Southern pine bark beetle.

At 2.3 miles, a trail splits left and climbs 0.5 mile to the summit of Furnace Mountain. The summit is covered with small chestnut oak, coppice chestnut, mountain laurel, blueberry, and huckleberry. At the top of the mountain, a small rock outcrop provides excellent views of Massanutten Mountain and the drainage of the Madison Run. For a pleasant day hike, return to the trailhead at this point.

If you're ready for more hiking, continue on the main trail through a small saddle. The grade eases, and the trail meets the Trayfoot Mountain Trail at 3.4 miles. Turn right on the Trayfoot Mountain Trail, which follows an old road south. The 0.2-mile climb to the 3,380-foot summit of Trayfoot Mountain is short but steep. There is also a trail junction at the summit. Take a right at the junction and continue southeast on a long descent down the ridge toward Paine Run. Blue blazes guide the way. The forest overstory gradually changes from the drier oak-hickory forest to cove hardwoods at Paine Run. About 3.8 miles from the summit of Trayfoot, the trail meets the Paine Run Trail at the creek. Turn left and hike up the run, passing near the results of a 1,400-acre forest fire that occurred in the fall of 1998.

The Paine Run Trail, marked with yellow blazes, follows an old road 3.5 miles to Skyline Drive. The climb is very gradual. The trail tops out at Black Rock Gap parking area at an elevation of 2,370 feet. Cross Skyline Drive and head north on the Appalachian Trail, which begins a gradual climb 0.7 mile to the Blackrock Hut AT Shelter.

Continue north 0.4 mile on the AT to join the Trayfoot Mountain Trail once again. The trails meet on the 3,092-foot summit of Black Rock amid a huge boulder field. A scramble to the top of the boulder field provides a tremendous view of the Shenandoah Valley. Turn left on the Trayfoot Mountain Trail and walk 0.1 mile east, then turn right at the next junction and continue another 0.9 mile to the Furnace Mountain Trail. Turn right on the Furnace Mountain Trail to return to your car at the trailhead.

APPENDIX A

Recommended Equipment for Backcountry Outings

Core essentials for day trips:

- day pack (or "day and a half" climbing-style pack, if needed)
- water: 2 quarts to 1 gallon per person per day (depending on season), in sturdy, screw-top plastic containers
- matches in a waterproof case, fire starter (commercially available fire sticks or pitch scraped off a dead tree and stored in a reclosable plastic bag)
- small first aid kit: tweezers, bandages, antiseptic, moleskin, snakebite kit
- insect repellent (in season)
- bee sting kit (over the counter antihistamine or epinephrine by prescription)
- sunglasses, sunblock, and lip sunscreen
- pocketknife
- whistle and mirror (for emergency signaling)
- flashlight with extra batteries and bulb (for those after-dark returns)
- lunch or snack, with bag for your trash
- toilet paper, with a plastic zipper bag to pack it out
- large-scale topo map and compass (be sure to adjust for magnetic declination)
- your FalconGuide
- sturdy, well-broken-in boots (normally light to medium weight)
- shirt, sweater, pants, and jacket suitable to the season
- socks: wool outer; light cotton, polypropylene, or nylon inner
- rain gear that can double as wind protection (breathable water-repellent parka and/or rain suit with pants or chaps)
- warm skiing-style hat (balaclava, headband, or stocking cap)
- hat, windproof with broad brim (for sun protection)
- gloves (weight depends on the season)
- belt and/or suspenders

If you're staying in the wilderness for one night or longer, add the following:

- backpack, pack cover, extra set of pack straps
- plastic bags (including a large garbage bag) with ties
- tent with fly and repair kit (including rip-stop tape)
- sleeping bag (rated to at least 10 degrees F or as season requires)
- sleeping pad (self-inflating type is best)
- stove, fuel bottle (filled), repair kit including cleaning wire
- candle lantern with spare candle

- cooking kit, pot gripper, cleaning pad
- eating utensils, including a bowl (12 to 15 ounces, with cover), cup, fork, spoon
- several small drawstring grab bags for miscellaneous items
- trowel
- biodegradable soap and small towel
- toothbrush, toothpaste, dental floss
- drugs: prescriptions and antibiotics
- zinc oxide (for treatment of sunburn)
- eye drops
- aspirin or ibuprofen
- throat lozenges
- laxatives
- decongestant medicine
- antacid tablets
- salt tablets
- scissors, safety pins, and small sewing kit
- moleskin (to prevent blistering), Second Skin (to treat blisters)
- extra bandages
- water filter designed and approved for backcountry use
- sharpening stone
- nylon cord, 50 to 100 feet (for hanging food, drying clothes, etc.)
- wading sandals or old running shoes that can be used around camp and for wading streams
- hiking shorts, swimsuit (summer)
- gaiters (especially for winter trips)
- undershirt and long underwear (polypropylene or capilene)

For winter trips add or substitute:

- internal frame backpack (lowers the center of gravity for better control on snowy or icy trails)
- space blanket
- extra shirt
- extra socks and underwear (3 to 5 pair for a weeklong trip)
- bandanna/handkerchiefs
- lightweight cotton or polypropylene gloves
- closed-cell foam pad (for insulation against the snow)
- foam pad for stove
- four-season tent

- sleeping bag rated to at least ‾10 degrees F (down-filled bag is best during winter)
- snow shovel
- ski accessories (extra tip, skins, wax, cork, and scrapper)
- transceivers (at least two in the party)
- warm, waterproof clothing that can be layered
- gallon-size plastic food storage bags (wear them in your boots over your socks to keep feet dry in slushy conditions)

Optional equipment for any day or overnight trip:

- compact binoculars
- camera, film, lens brush, and paper
- walking stick (especially useful for probing muddy stream bottoms)
- notebook and pencils
- book
- field guides
- fishing tackle (fly and/or spin)

So there you have it—80 pounds of lightweight gear! Actually, most people can get along safely and comfortably with 35 to 50 pounds of gear and food, depending on the duration of the trip. Your pack will weigh 8 to 10 pounds more during winter with four-season gear and heavier clothing.

APPENDIX B

Virginia Conservation Organizations

Appalachian Trail Conference
799 Washington Street
P.O. Box 807
Harpers Ferry, WV 25425
(304) 535–6331
www.atconf.org

Clinch Coalition
4034-A Dungannon Road
Coeburn, VA 24230
(276) 395–2057
www.clinchcoalition.org
delta@naxs.com

National Parks and Conservation Association
1776 Massachusetts Avenue, NW
Washington, DC 20036
(800) NAT–PARK or (202) 223–6722
www.npca.org
npca@npca.org

The Nature Conservancy
1233 A Cedars Court
Charlottesville, VA 22903
(804) 295–6106
Fax: (804) 979–0370
www.nature.org
rriordan@tnc.org

The Nature Conservancy
Virginia Coast Reserve
P.O. Box 158
Nassawadox, VA 23413
(757) 442–3049
www.nature.org

Terry Thompson,
tathompson@esva.net

Sierra Club, Virginia Chapter
6 North Sixth Street
Richmond, VA 23219
(804) 225–9113
Fax: (804) 225–9114
www.virginia.sierraclub.org

There are thirteen local chapters of the Sierra Club:

- Appalachian Highlands (Bristol)
- Battlefields (Fredericksburg)
- Blue Ridge (Faber)
- Chesapeake Bay (Virginia Beach)
- Falls of the James (Richmond)
- Great Falls (Vienna)
- Mount Vernon (Alexandria)
- New River (Blacksburg)
- Piedmont (Charlottesville)
- Roanoke River (Roanoke)
- Shenandoah (Harrisonburg)
- Thunder Ridge (Lynchburg)
- York River (Gloucester)

Southern Appalachian Forest Coalition
46 Haywood Street, Suite 323
Asheville, NC 28801
(828)252–9223
www.safc.org

Southern Environmental Law Center
201 West Main Street, Suite 14
Charlottesville, VA 22902

(434) 977–4090
www.selcva.org
selcva@selcva.org

Virginia Natural Heritage Program
217 Governor Street, Third Floor
Richmond, VA 23219
(804) 786–7951
Fax: (804) 371–2674
www.dcr.state.va.us/dnh/index.html
Megan Rollins, mgr@dcr.state.va.us

Virginia Wilderness Committee
Route 1, Box 319
Mount Crawford, VA 22841
Contact Lynn Cameron, (540)
234–6273
www.jmu.edu/users/camerosl/wild/
  wild.htm
camerosl@jmu.edu

The Wilderness Society
900 Seventeenth Street N.W.
Washington, DC 20006-2506
(800) THE–WILD
www.wilderness.org

**The Wilderness Society's
Southeastern Region**
1447 Peachtree Street, NE
Suite 812
Atlanta, GA 30309-3029
(404) 872–9453
www.wilderness.org/ccc/southeast
George Gay, ggay@tws.org

Appalachian Trail Maintainance Clubs:

Mount Rogers A.T. Club
24198 Green Spring Road
Abingdon, VA 24211-5320
www.geocities.com/Yosemite/Geyser/
  2539/
Pat Hensley, loonyhiker@pipeline.com
56.2 miles, Damascus, VA to VA 670

Natural Bridge A.T. Club
P.O. Box 3012
Lynchburg, VA 24503
www.nbatc.org
Bill Foot, HappiFeet@aol.com
87.9 miles, Blackhorse Gap (FR 186)
  to Tye River (VA 664)

Old Dominion A.T. Club
P.O. Box 25283
Richmond, VA 23260
www.odatc.org
John Reilly, cvkr39a@prodigy.com
17 miles, Reeds Gap (VA 664) to
  Rockfish Gap (I–64)

Piedmont A.T. Hikers
Piedmont Appalachian Trail Hikers
P.O. Box 4423
Greensbors, NC 27404–4423
www.path-at.org/
path@path-at.org
57 miles, VA 670 to Garden
  Mountain (VA 623)

Potomac A.T. Club
118 Park Street, S.E.
Vienna, VA 22180
(703) 242–0315
www.patc.net
Heidi Forrest, heidif@erols.com
240 miles, Rockfish Gap (I–64) to
   Pine Grove Furnace State Park,
   Pennsylvania

Roanoke A.T. Club
P.O. Box 12282
Roanoke, VA 24024
131.2 miles, Lickskillet Hollow (VA
   608) to Blackhorse Gap (FR 186)

Tidewater A.T. Club
P.O. Box 8246
Norfolk, VA 23503
www.tidewateratc.com
jsexton@erols.com,
davemims@videoatlantic.com
9.9 miles, Tye River (VA 56) to
   Reeds Gap (VA 664)

Virginia Tech Outing Club
P.O. Box 538
Blacksburg, VA 24060
www.vt.edu:10021/org/outing/index.
   html
crabidea@vt.edu
29.6 miles, Garden Mountain (VA
   623) to Lickskillet Hollow (VA
   608)

APPENDIX C

Virginia Land Management Agencies

Blacksburg Ranger District
110 Southpark Drive
Blacksburg, VA 24060
(540) 552–4641

Clinch Ranger District
9416 Darden Drive
Wise, VA 24293
(276) 328–2931

Deerfield Ranger District
Route 6, Box 419
Staunton, VA 24401
(540) 885–8028

Dry River Ranger District
112 North River Road
Bridgewater, VA 22812
(540) 828–2591

Glenwood/Pedlar Ranger District
P.O. Box 10
Natural Bridge Station, VA 24579
(540) 291–2189

Highlands Gateway Visitor Center
Factory Merchants Mall, Drawer B-12
Max Meadows, VA 24360
(800) 446–9670

James River Ranger District
810-A Madison Avenue
Covington, VA 24426
(540) 962–2214

Jefferson and Washington National Forest
5162 Valleypointe Parkway
Roanoke, VA 24019-3050
(888) 265–0019 or (540) 265–5100
www.southernregion.fs.fed.us/gwj/
pao/r8_gwjeff@fs.fed.us

Lee Ranger District
109 Molineu Road
Edinburg, VA 22824
(540) 984–4101

Massanutten Visitor's Center
Route 1, Box 100
New Market, VA 22844
(540) 740–8310

Mount Rogers National Recreation Area
3714 Highway 16
Marion, VA 24354-4097
(276) 783–5196

New Castle Ranger District
Box 246
New Castle, VA 24127
(540) 864–5195

Shenandoah National Park
3655 US 211 East
Luray, VA 22835
(540) 999–3500
www.nps.gov/shen

Warm Springs Ranger District
Highway 220 South
Route 2, Box 30
Hot Springs, VA 24445
(540) 839–2521

Wythe Ranger District
155 Sherwood Road
Wytheville, VA 24382
(276) 228–5551

**Virginia Department of Game and
  Inland Fisheries**
4010 West Broad Street
Richmond, VA 23230
(804) 367–1000
www.dgif.state.va.us/index.cfm
dgifweb@dgif.state.va.us

APPENDIX D

Topo Map Index

1 Little River Roadless Area
Palo Alto
Reddish Knob
Stokesville
West Augusta

2 Ramsey's Draft Wilderness
McDowell
Palo Alto
West Augusta

3 Crawford Mountain Roadless Area
Churchville
Elliot Knob
Stokesville
West Augusta

4 Laurel Fork Special Management Area
Thornwood
Snowy Mountain

5 Rough Mountain Wilderness
Longdale Furnace
Nimrod Hall

6 Rich Hole Wilderness/Mill Mountain Roadless Area
Collierstown
Longdale Furnace
Millboro
Nimrod Hall

7 Three Ridges Wilderness
Big Levels
Horseshoe Mountain
Massie Mill
Sherando

8 The Priest Wilderness
Massies Mill

9 Saint Marys Wilderness
Big Levels
Vesuvius

10 Adams Peak Roadless Area
Cornwall
Montbello
Vesuvius

11 Mount Pleasant National Scenic Area
Forks Of Buffalo
Montbello

12 Three Sisters Roadless Area
Buena Vista
Glasgow
Snowden

13 Barbours Creek Wilderness
Jordan Mines
New Castle
Potts Creek

14 Shawvers Run Wilderness
Potts Creek

15 Mountain Lake Wilderness
Eggleston
Interior
Newport
Waiteville

16 Cascades Roadless Area
Eggleston

17 Peters Mountain Wilderness
Interior
Lindside

18 Kimberling Creek Wilderness
Rocky Gap

19 Brushy Mountain
Bland
Rocky Gap

20 Little Walker Mountain Roadless Area
Long Spur
Pulaski

21 Beartown Wilderness
Hutchinson Rock

22 Lewis Fork Wilderness
Troutdale
White Top Mountain

23 Little Wilson Creek Wilderness
Troutdale

24 Little Dry Run Wilderness
Cedar Springs
Speedwell

25 North Creek Roadless Area
Peaks of Otter

26 Thunder Ridge Wilderness
Arnold Valley
Snowden

27 James River Face Wilderness
Snowden

28 Virginia Coastal Preserve
Accomac
Bloxom
Cheriton
Cobb Island
Metompkin Inlet
Nassawadox
Quinby Inlet
Townsend
Ship Shoal Inlet
Wachapreague
Wallops Island
GMCO Map of the Barrier
Islands (not 1:24,000)

29 North River Landing Nature Preserve
Pleasant Ridge
Creeds

30 Shenandoah National Park

Shenandoah National Park Maps,
1:62,500 scale, available as
northern, central, and southern
sections. 1:24,000 scale maps:
Greenfield
Waynesboro West
Waynesboro East
Crozet
Fort Defiance
Crimora
Browns Cove
Free Union
Grottoes
McGayheysville
Swift Run Gap
Standardsville
Rochelle
Elkton West

Elkton East
Fletcher
Madison
Brightwood
Stanley
Big Meadows
Old Rag Mountain
Woodville
Luray
Thornton Gap
Washington
Massies Corner
Rileyville
Bentonville
Chester Gap
Flint Hill
Strasburg
Front Royal

ABOUT THE AUTHORS

Mark Miller is employed by the Southern Appalachian Forest Coalition and is working to protect and preserve roadless and wilderness lands in Virginia's National Forests. He and his wife, Cindy, live in Lexington, Virginia, with their three daughters. Mark began hiking in northern Minnesota at a young age. He has hiked extensively in Montana, North Carolina, and Virginia. In addition to hiking, his other interests include bicycling and gardening.

Steven Carroll grew up in Virginia and has hiked there his entire life. Raised in Alleghany County, Steven and his wife, Gina, now tackle hikes from their home base in Lexington, Kentucky. Aside from hiking, Steven enjoys fly-fishing, mountain biking, and photography. A University of Virginia graduate, Steven works as a field geologist for an environmental consultant.

Mark and Steven have collaborated on two other hiking guides: *Hiking West Virginia* and *Fine Trails of Rockbridge*.

FALCON GUIDES®

From nature exploration to extreme adventure, FalconGuides lead you there. With more than 400 titles available, there is a guide for every outdoor activity and topic, including essential outdoor skills, field identification, trails, trips, and the best places to go in each state and region. Written by experts, each guidebook features detailed descriptions, maps, and advice that can enhance every outdoor experience.

You can count on FalconGuides to lead you to your favorite outdoor activities wherever you live or travel.

WILD GUIDES

Published in cooperation with The Wilderness Society

Wildlands offer excellent opportunities for exploration and recreation in more secluded areas. These books provide the information you need to get off the beaten path and into the wildest backcountry and wild areas across America.

6" x 9" · paperback · maps

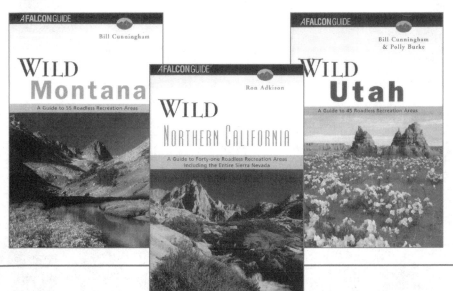

WHAT'S SO SPECIAL ABOUT UNSPOILED, NATURAL PLACES?

Beauty   Solitude   Wildness   Freedom   Quiet   Adventure
Serenity   Inspiration   Wonder   Excitement
Relaxation   Challenge

There's a lot to love about our treasured public lands, and the reasons are different for each of us. Whatever your reasons are, the national **Leave No Trace** education program will help you discover special outdoor places, enjoy them, and preserve them—today and for those who follow. By practicing and passing along these simple principles, you can help protect the special places you love from being loved to death.

THE PRINCIPLES OF LEAVE NO TRACE

- Plan ahead and prepare
- Travel and camp on durable surfaces
- Dispose of waste properly
- Leave what you find
- Minimize campfire impacts
- Respect wildlife
- Be considerate of other visitors

Leave No Trace is a national nonprofit organization dedicated to teaching responsible outdoor recreation skills and ethics to everyone who enjoys spending time outdoors.

To learn more or to become a member, please visit us at www.LNT.org or call (800) 332-4100.

Leave No Trace, P.O. Box 997, Boulder, CO 80306